12 R/S

001486
9780582105331

D1799221

 LONDON BOROUGH OF LEWISHAM
LIBRARY SERVICE

Author

Title

BOOK STORE

The Tide of Divorce

William Latey Q C

The Tide of Divorce

With a Foreword by
The Right Hon. Lord Denning, Master of the Rolls

 LONGMAN

£ 2.25

582 10533 1

To my dear sons John and Maurice
staunch friends ever

LONGMAN GROUP LIMITED
London
Associated companies, branches and
representatives throughout the world

First published 1970

SBN 582 105331

Printed in Great Britain at
the University Press, Aberdeen

Contents

Foreword

The Right Hon. Lord Denning, Master of the Rolls

We have been brought up to believe in the institution of marriage. It is the basis of family life which is the foundation of society. The Christian concept of it is a lifelong union of one man with one woman. Yet this very institution is threatened today. Young people are asking whether it is so sacred as their parents used to believe. Well may they ask it.

In our lifetime divorces have increased twentyfold, thirtyfold, nay a hundredfold. Divorce used to be disreputable. Its participants were regarded as outcasts. Now it is respectable and its adherents are accepted everywhere. No one condemns divorce—rather applauds it as a proper end to a marriage that has broken down. So much so that some of the younger generation seek to revive the ideal of Plato's republic in which men and women come together to procreate children as members of a community without any individual family life—a community in which no child will know its own father.

The institution of marriage may look to them as a castle built in sand which is being eaten away by the encroaching tide of divorce and only waits for the next big wave or two before it is washed away.

William Latey has watched the approaching tide with apprehension. In this book he traces its course and he illumines it with spotlights. He throws into relief the plight of Queens. He tells of the discarded Catherine of Aragon. He picks out the flirtations of Caroline of Brunswick. His eyes light on the private Bills of Divorce that used to be laid before Parliament with all the incidents of adultery detailed without any reticence! He tells the history of Royal Commissions and their Reports of acts of Parliament and their consequences. The book is not a heavy history of events. It is a story-book which both fascinates and instructs.

Towards the end 'Bill' Latey—as he is affectionately known—does not conceal his concern at the new Divorce Reform Act which allows divorce for 'irretrievable breakdown' of marriage. He ends it with the ominous prophecy: 'The tide of divorce will rise rapidly and may overflow.' All good folk will hope that this prophecy will not come true. For the sake of our civilisation, we hope that the tide will turn. For, after all is said and done, the future of the country depends on the way in which children are brought up. They are best brought up in the happiness and security of a sound family life. This in turn rests on the maintenance of the institution of marriage.

In this book the author has drawn on a lifetime of experience in the law of divorce. He has written this short history of divorce which is without equal. It is well worth reading by all concerned with the rising 'tide of divorce'.

DENNING

Preface

At no time in history has divorce affected more families than today in England and in most other countries professing Christianity. As a humble chronicler I have tried to tell the story of marriage and divorce from the earliest recorded times. As one whose professional career has been spent mainly in the English divorce court as counsel and judge I may be excused perhaps for describing so fully the development of the divorce law in England.

Each era of our island history has seen changes, mostly for the better, in social habits and conditions, and it has seemed desirable to give a glimpse of the background in which our marriage and divorce laws were framed from time to time. In so doing I have borrowed largely from historians whose weighty words will echo through the corridors of time.

Divorce as we understand it, i.e. the lawful disruption of the marriage bond, was common in early Roman law, and continued, with modifications from time to time until in the Christian era marriage was declared indissoluble save by death of one of the spouses. The ecclesiastical courts under the Pope only had the power of dealing with matrimonial causes, and established for centuries a system of annulments of marriage on grounds that were far-fetched, almost to a ridiculous extent. Thus under the Canon Law of Rome many divorces were decreed under the name of nullity. As time went on, however, a number of the more fictitious or obsolescent grounds of nullity were dropped, but divorce as such is still not allowed in countries like Italy and

Spain in which the Roman Canon Law is exercised, although the Italian House of Deputies has recently passed a measure for limited divorce.

These developments are traced in this book, which moreover stresses the drastic change brought about by the Reformation in Henry VIII's reign, whereby Papal jurisdiction was abolished in England. Yet only judicial separation continued here, similar to the Roman divorce *a mensa et thoro*, from bed and board; and this went on in England till the Act of 1857, subject to Parliamentary private Acts of Divorce, only available to rich people. The Reformation, due to a popular dislike of Papal dues and to Henry VIII's desperate but successful efforts to get rid of his lawful wife, Catherine of Aragon, made such a mark in history that a chapter has been devoted to the case of his hapless wife.

The many Royal Commissions and Government Committees which have been appointed since 1853 to consider the problems of divorce and jurisdiction in matrimonial causes have one and all emphasised the national importance of maintaining the institution of marriage as a lifelong union, and regarding divorce as a species of safety-valve in the case of marriages hopelessly broken by matrimonial offences of one spouse or the other. Equality of the sexes having been laid down as regards the offence of adultery by an Act in 1923, it was not until the Matrimonial Causes Act, 1937, initiated by Sir Alan Herbert, that the grounds of divorce were enlarged, available to husband or wife. These were adultery, cruelty and desertion, with sundry other offences not of frequent occurrence. In England Parliament has passed the Divorce Reform Act 1969 substituting for the pre-existing grounds of divorce a single ground under the heading of 'irretrievable breakdown of marriage', coupled with divorce by mutual consent of the parties and also divorce after five years' separation with or without the consent of the other party to the marriage.

The consequences of these changes, for good or ill of English society and family life, cannot be foreseen, but in the author's opinion they are important enough to justify a review of the arguments put forward for and against, contained in the last three chapters.

Whether the lessons of history in the Christian world are anything to go by in the changing habits and customs of the present day must be left to serious thinkers on this subject.

Owing to the admitted need of strengthening the financial protection of wives and children the operation of the Act was deferred until 1 January 1971, to give time for a separate Government Bill for that purpose to be passed.

WILLIAM LATEY

January 1970

1 In Ancient Eras

Marriage and divorce! The one conjures up a young couple bent on a happy future together, with the vision of children to love and be loved; the other a phantasmagoria of broken pledges, perhaps broken hearts, a broken link—and freedom to try again. Maybe that worldly-wise and scholarly lawyer Francis Bacon was not entranced with his own marriage when a year later he wrote in his Essay on Marriage and Single Life: 'He was reputed one of the wise men that made answer to the question, When a man should marry? *A young man not yet; an elder man not at all.*' But he was not an ordinary mortal, and, deeply in debt, he married money. To moralise on the causes of divorce is in vain, but the ebb and flow of divorce from early times is not without its lessons.

Much of the modern laws in Europe and this country derive from Roman customs and the all-pervading influence of the Roman adoption of the Christian religion. But before Rome founded a settled civilisation there existed in Europe, and in the Near East, a system of family law which has been illumined in the English language by the famous work of Sir Henry Maine, and in German by Rudolf von Ihering. Primitive society left little in the way of recording the system of marriage as we understand it nowadays. The family was the social unit, ruled by the patriarch who had despotic power over its members, even for life or death. Divorce in the modern sense was unknown, because the patriarch could put away any member of the family at will, whether or not there had been a formal union or a loose partnership. Thus came the *patria potestas* of early Greek and Roman eras.

Plutarch tells us how marriages were celebrated in Lacedaemonia many centuries before the advent of Christ. The man carried off his bride by a pretence of violence. He placed her on a bed, untied her girdle and carried her to another bed. After several nights of wooing they consummated the union. So important was the propagation of a family that if no children were born a husband in Sparta could lend his wife to another man for that purpose, such adultery not being considered an offence. In the reign of Lycurgus, when the Spartan wars took away so many young men, women gained much more freedom and domestic power.

Those among us today who look askance at nudist camps would be surprised by the habit, sanctioned by Lycurgus, of young maidens appearing naked on special festivals in the presence of naked young men, and dancing and singing without any element of disgrace. The purpose was not only to accustom young people to the sight of the unclothed human body but to incline those taking part to love and marriage.

Going further back into the mists of time we read in Genesis: 'God created man in his own image . . . male and female created He them: and God blessed them and said unto them: be fruitful and multiply.' Follows the evolution of Eve from Adam's rib, and the passage: 'Therefore shall a man leave his father and his mother, and shall cleave unto his wife; and they shall be one flesh. And they were both naked, the man and his wife, and were not ashamed.' Thus we have the first marriage in biblical history, with Cain, a tiller of the ground, and Abel, a keeper of sheep, as the progeny.

Maine points out that the earliest notions of a law or rule of life were contained in the Homeric word Themis, the goddess of justice, the Themistes being the judges' awards, the result of divine inspiration. The Hindu Manu conception of a diety's dictating a body of law arose later. Early mankind, said Maine, imagined a divine personal agent for the forces of nature—the wind blowing, the sun rising and setting, and the earth yielding her increase. Nevertheless this notion hardly affected family relations. As already indicated the male head of the family, or *gens*, had supreme power over wives and children. It was a sacred duty to beget children in marriage.

As Roman rule gradually developed with its zeal, as the centuries passed, for orderly government, the root notion of marriage as a legal bond took shape. For centuries the *patria potestas* held sway, the wife more or less the chattel of her husband (in *manu mariti*), except that a Roman patrician who married a plebeian was debarred the absolute right over his wife or of *patria potestas* over their children; a woman married thus (*sine manu*), could still be claimed by her father if he chose to demand her return to him. In 445 B.C. Caius Canuleius swept away any distinction between the two orders in regard to lawful marriage. Before the last days of the Roman Republic (27 B.C.) the patriarchal system had died out and was replaced by divorce on the basis of dissolution by mutual consent or even by the will of one spouse. But under Augustus (27 B.C.) a stricter code was introduced.

With paganism and worship of the gods still prevailing in early Roman times daily prayers were uttered by orthodox families for the ancestors. Assembled before the altar at which fire was kept alight the worshippers said their prayers. As Aeschylus (525–455 B.C.) wrote in *The Supplicants*: 'Let the altars blaze, and each due rite propitiate every god to avert the evil.' Nor was this form of worship limited to ceremonial occasions. In a picturesque passage in *The Last Days of Pompeii* (1834) Bulwer Lytton describes the meeting of Glaucus and Ione in the temple of Minerva at Neapolis. Both of Athenian origin, they paid tribute to their ancestors and together laid their olive garlands on the altar, after touching the knee of their goddess. For Glaucus and his beloved Ione this temple meeting was the beginning of a romance which survived the disaster of Pompeii.[1]

Even in Nero's time whole families turned out for a religious ceremonial not unlike the harvest festival of today, except that it was to placate the gods. Swine were sacrificed, garlands were

[1] Pompeii was destroyed by the Vesuvius eruption in A.D. 27.

3

worn, corn was thrown into fire. In A.D. 391 the Emperor Theodosius prohibited pagan cults and made the Christian faith the
state religion, but heathen rites lingered on. The religious ritual
was reflected in the ceremony of marriage. Before that among
patricians came the betrothal, and preceding the marriage ceremonial the auspices were taken to invoke the gods' blessing of
the union (see Cicero, *De Div.* 1.46). A beast was sacrificed, with
some form of vegetable offering with the notion of promoting
fertility. The bride discarded her dolls and toys, and changed her
dress to a pure white toga and woollen tunic, encircled by a
woollen belt. Her hair was arranged in six locks with woollen
bands, and her head covered by a red veil, supposed to reflect
the sacred fire of her new home, and surmounted by a wreath of
flowers. There came a further sacrifice of beasts when the couple's
hands were joined. All present carried garlands.

After the wedding banquet followed the bride's farewell to her
old home. She was taught to make a show of resistance at this
point, being taken from her mother's arms. With her husband and
a rejoicing procession of relations and guests, singing chants, she
was taken to her new home. At the entrance she anointed the door
with swine's fat as a symbol of fertility. The groom gave her a
coin in token of her dowry, and made a similar offering to propitiate
the household gods. He lifted his bride over the threshold. In this
ancient pagan ceremony lies the origin of the taste still existing in
the twentieth century for a white wedding and all its accompani-
ments, though nowadays the custom of lifting the bride over the
threshold of her new home is a rare occurrence.

When the Roman civil law developed under the Republic there
was little change in marriage customs. Patricians favoured the
ceremony of *conferreatio,* so named from the use of a sacred cake of
salted rice, *far.* Ten witnesses attended, if the bridal pair belonged
to different families. Another form of marriage under the Roman
civil law was styled *coemptio* (a relic of the ancient practice of bride
purchase) in the presence of a balance-holder with copper scales.
Gibbon describes how the bride fulfilled the coemption by buying
with three pieces of copper her entry to her husband's house and
household deities. At the ceremony the spouses were seated on

sheepskins. This form was mainly used by plebeians. The couple expressed their consent to the marriage before five witnesses. The bride renounced her own family and was given the status of the daughter of her husband and the sister of her own children. Her husband had the power of life and death over her for adultery or drunkenness, and whatever property she had became his. Nevertheless the wife usually had supreme domestic influence in her home.

Later came the form of *usucapio* whereby if a man and woman lived together for a year or more they were deemed to be properly married, not unlike our presentday marriage by habit and repute, which, however, necessitates proof of a presumed ceremony of marriage. But the wife could interrupt *usucapio* by absenting herself for three days, *trinoctium*.

After the Punic Wars, ending with the final defeat of the Carthaginians by the Roman legions in the second century B.C., women began to agitate against the ancient nuptial ceremonies, and marriage contracts were agreed upon, whereby they could retain their own property, a foretaste of *séparation des biens*, subject to parental consent.

Under the civil law of the Republic the requisites of marriage were *connubium*, meaning liberty to marry if not forbidden by the somewhat complex rules of relationship, modified in later times; age, fourteen for a male, twelve for a female; and the consent of the person under whose power the would-be spouses lived, as well as of the parties.

Already in 449 B.C. the Twelve Tables had been issued under the rules of the Decemviri, the most famous of the early law codes, but they did little to change the existing obligations of marriage or family relations. When divorce entered into Roman law a marriage could be dissolved by the consent of husband or wife. It differed from the practice of *Repudium* whereby the husband could cast off his wife on the ground of some grievous misconduct as interpreted in that epoch; whether unchastity or adultery or drunkenness, or even if the wife went to a public place without her husband's leave. Even trifling indiscretions by a wife were visited on occasion with grotesque severity by husbands. The husband was not entitled to kill his wife unless she was caught in adultery—*in flagrante delicto*—in which case he could kill the lover; and unless she had been guilty of immorality he had still to maintain her. *Repudium* involved no judicial decision, except that a domestic forum was summoned in some cases. The formula used by the husband to the wife was 'I take away thy property and call upon thee to restore the house keys to me.'

In 17 B.C. the Lex Julia de Adulteriis brought into being a more formal procedure for *repudium*. The husband presented his wife with a tablet recording the act, much in the same way as a Jewish Ghet, in the presence of seven witnesses. By the end of the Republic no public ceremony for marriage was required, except certain customary ceremonials. Divorce had become a private matter between the spouses, and only when a dispute arose about property or the care of children did a judicial inquiry follow. On divorce the wife lost her husband's domicile. Divorce was allowed *inter alia* on the grounds of serious disease such as leprosy and insanity.

Though monogamy was the custom, concubinage by a husband was not frowned upon, and indeed continued until the tenth century A.D. There was no judicial divorce, it being consensual or even at the will of one spouse, subject to the assent of the paterfamilias. Widows were at first forbidden to marry again, but later a delay of nine to ten months before remarriage was prescribed in case of issue by the first husband after his death.

In the first ages [wrote Gibbon] the father of a family might sell his children, and his wife was reckoned in the number of his children; the domestic judge might pronounce the death of an offender or his mercy might expel her from his bed and board; but the slavery of the wretched female was hopeless and perpetual unless he asserted for his own convenience the prerogative of divorce. . . . When the Roman matrons became the equal and voluntary companions of their lords, a new jurisprudence was introduced, that marriage like other partnerships might be dissolved by the abdication of one of the associates.

6

Whether or not the loose law of marriage and its easy dissolution led to the decay of society, the last two centuries of the Republic were marked by a widespread corruption of morals, in which the vagaries of married women played almost as important a part as those of their husbands. The prevailing notion was that marriage being dependent on mutual affection if that ceased either spouse could divorce the other. Gibbon says that three centuries of prosperity and corruption led to:

the most tender of human connections being degraded to a transient society of profit and pleasure . . . Both sexes alternately felt the disgrace and injury; an inconstant spouse transferred her wealth to a new family, abandoning a numerous, perhaps a spurious, progeny to the paternal authority and care of her late husband. . . . The matron who in five years can submit to the embraces of eight husbands must cease to reverence the chastity of her own person.

There is some doubt whether this last reference, drawn from Juvenal, always hard on the society women of his day, was not farfetched.

However, there is more than a glimpse of high society as it was little changed in the first century A.D. in the satires of Juvenal (A.D. 55–130), and the *Satyricon* of Petronius. A shrewd administrator, he became Nero's mentor till he fell from the Emperor's favour, after indulging his own and his master's gross licentiousness at orgies in which the love of boys played no small part. Women in the upper classes were wont to marry to gain freedom to live as they liked, to choose their lovers, sometimes from the ranks of the gladiators. And homosexual men married to escape the then penalties for celibacy. Jack Lindsay in his historical novel, *Thunder Underground* (Muller, 1965), set in the reign of Nero, described how a much divorced lady is congratulated by her friends on a fresh betrothal. Nevertheless good-living wives suffered most from the freedom of divorce until reforms were gradually introduced during the Christian era.

With the advent of the Roman Empire and Julius Caesar (60–44

7

B.C.) scarcely any change was made in the laws of marriage and divorce. Paganism still survived; but the old marriage methods of *coemptio, confarreatio* and *usus* fell into disuse, together with that of the wife passing in *manum*, with the result that married women had an equal right of divorce at will with their husbands, although economic considerations often restricted such freedom of action. In the second century A.D. the rights of the paterfamilias were extinguished.

It was not until the code of the Emperor Justinian came into force (A.D. 528–564) that the principle of divorce by mutual consent was narrowed down. Divorce could be had on the grounds of a man's impotence subject to a triennial period of delay; retirement to a monastery; and prolonged captivity. The more important grounds were a wife's treason or concealing from her husband plots against the state, her absences against his will, and abortion. The wife could divorce her husband on the first two grounds, also if he tried to make her commit adultery, or if he consorted with another woman. Nevertheless the great social evil of capricious divorce was only a little mitigated despite the Imperial edicts.

Prior to the Justinian code the Christian faith was developing in the Roman Empire. In A.D. 323 the Emperor Constantine adopted it, and he decreed the destruction of the heathen temples, but he did not abolish divorce by mutual consent though laying down certain modifications with penalties for disobedience, such as inhibition against marrying again and the wife having to be confined in a monastery, and deprived of her separate property, part of which accrued to the monastery. His successors, Emperors Theodosius and Valentinian, paid special regard to the interests of children in the event of divorce. These restrictions on freedom of divorce did not coincide with public opinion and Justin, who succeeded Justinian in A.D. 565, re-enacted divorce by mutual consent; and it was not until the eighth century A.D. that Leo (of the Eastern Empire) forbade consensual divorces, thus paving the way to the more rigid canon law.

As Holdsworth points out[1] from the beginning of the Holy

[1] *History of English Law*, Vol. 1, *Ecclesiastical Courts*, Methuen, 1922 (3rd ed.), p. 580.

8

Roman Empire with the coronation of Charles the Great by Pope Leo III in A.D. 800 Western Europe accepted the Roman Emperor as ruling in matters temporal and the Pope in matters spiritual. This principle was carried on by the German Emperors in the tenth century, dominating Western Europe till the Renaissance and the English Reformation. For centuries any important appeal from the sentence of an ecclesiastical court was heard in Rome, and in the thirteenth century more English cases came before the Papal tribunal than from any other country.

2 Canon Law of Rome

Canon, of Greek origin, came to mean model of excellence as laid down by the Christian scriptures. Under the ecclesiastical domination of the laws of marriage, which by degrees passed from the civil power to that of the popes of Rome, marriage became indissoluble. Though the term *divortium a vinculo* was usual, it really meant nullity of marriage. The procedure was used in the historic case of Henry VIII of England and his first wife Catherine of Aragon; it really amounted to a decree of nullity (see Chapter 4).

The Canon Law of Rome developed into a body of legislation which eventually took the place of the civil law, and was based on the ecclesiastical view of Christian principles. These principles were derived from fear of the supposed vice of sexual communion, which was regarded as sinful unless for the purpose of procreation; and treatment of marriage as a holy sacrament. At first only Christian couples were subject to the ecclesiastical rules, but when Christianity became universal all were affected. The first body of canons was compiled in the sixth century A.D., about the time of Justinian. But at the end of the ninth century A.D. the Church took further hold with its canons, often confusing, until the Abbot Gratian completed his code *Concordantia Discordantium Canonum* in the twelfth century. Whereas the requisite of just marriage in the civil law had been consent and not cohabitation in the sexual sense (*non cubitus sed consensus facit*), Gratian laid it down that both were necessary. At last came the *Corpus Juris Canonici* with the

Church in complete control of marriage and divorce. The official version of the *Corpus* was issued by Pope Gregory XIII in 1582. It must be remembered that in those days the lawyers were nearly all ecclesiasts, and they developed and changed the matrimonial civil law as time passed.

Divorce at will or by mutual consent was abolished. Marriage was a lifelong union which could not be dissolved except by death. But an escape valve was kept open by the very wide principles governing nullity of marriage, whereby a ceremony of marriage could be declared void for reasons, good or bad. The Church created the system of divorce *a mensa et thoro* (equivalent to our judicial separation) on the grounds of adultery, perverse practices, cruelty, heresy and apostasy; but the spouses remained lawfully married.

It was the wives who mostly had to suffer the misdoing of their husbands. The early Christian fathers gave married women a low status as compared with their husbands with regard to divorce. St Augustine of Hippo (A.D. 354–430) whose later principles after a sensual life induced him to regard his own marriage with regret, yet regarded polygamy and prostitution as necessary to men 'as a sewer is to a palace'. He looked upon marriage as a means of avoiding promiscuous sexual intercourse, but thought that a wife should 'endure joyfully her lord's debaucheries and ill-treatment'. Finally he decided that marriage was indissoluble. St Jerome (A.D. 340–420) a great scholar among the early Christian fathers who lived an ascetic life at the monastery which he founded at Bethlehem for many years, and translated the Bible into the Latin Vulgate, was unduly severe on women who married again after divorce in terms which in these days would be regarded as extremely indelicate.

There is an oft-quoted dialogue between a protesting and a submissive wife in the *Familiarium Colloquiae Conjugium* of Erasmus. The rebellious wife Xantippe complains to her recently married friend Eulalia, of her husband's vicious habits and his cruelty, and of his miserliness over her dress, making her put up with rags, like the British.

Eulalia   But British wool is the same colour as Venetian.

Xantippe laments further her tattered rags, and says she would sooner live with a pig and intends to leave her husband, a monster who has assaulted her with a stool and threatened to turn her out. She complains that he has spent her dowry and of his drunkenness and spending whole nights away from her.

Eulalia blamed her for such abuse of her lord and master. It was not right to talk like that.

X   Not right! If he does not treat me as his wife I shall not look upon him as a husband.

E   But Peter and Paul say that we must obey our husbands, and Sarah called her husband 'lord'.

X   But Paul says that men should love their wives. When he does his duty I shall do mine, not while he treats me as a servant.

E   Whatever your husband is like, you have no right to change and get another. Now divorce has been abolished, you will have to remain married to your husband to the end of your days.

X   It was some infernal fiend who took that right from us.

E   It was Christ who did it.

It is of course a fact that the canon law with its principle of indissolubility of marriage based itself on certain statements attributed to our Lord in the gospels. Innumerable theses have been written about what principles He did lay down, having regard to the somewhat inconsistent sayings attributed to Christ by the apostles and to Jewish customs in this epoch. Ancient biblical history has been invoked to the contrary, such as the reference in Deuteronomy 24: 1. 'When a man hath taken a wife, and married her, and it come to pass that she find no favour in his eyes, because he hath found some uncleanness in her: then let him write her a bill of divorcement and give it in her hand, and send her out of his house. And when she is departed out of his house she may go and be another man's wife.'

And coming to the New Testament the well known saying of Christ to the Pharisees in Mark 10 when He was asked 'Is it lawful for a man to put away his wife?' He answered, 'What did Moses command you?' and they said: 'Moses suffered to write a bill of divorcement, and to put her away.' Christ answered: 'For the hardness of your heart he wrote you this precept. But from the beginning of the creation God made them male and female. For this cause shall a man leave his father and mother, and cleave to his wife; and they twain shall be one flesh . . . What, therefore, God hath joined together, let not man put asunder.'

Next He told His disciples, 'Whosoever shall put away his wife, and marry another, committeth adultery against her. And if a woman shall put away her husband, and be married to another, she committeth adultery.'

From this passage in St Mark and other sentences in the writings of the apostles was derived the principle of indissolubility of marriage under the canon law. Reams have been written about Christ's actual meaning and whether adultery justified divorce in His view. One of the most recent dissertations on this subject was that contained in the 1955 Report of the Archbishops' Commission on the Law of Nullity of marriage. After quoting the references by the apostles and by St Paul in his Epistles, the Report says: 'We are unanimous in our opinion that in the New Testament the principle of the permanence of the marriage bond is unequivocally affirmed.'[1]

In all these theses written by learned divines and scholars and by secular students through the ages about the true and proper interpretation of Christ's meanings on particular occasions, perhaps a passage in Sir George Grey's speech in the House of Commons on the Matrimonial Causes Bill in 1857 may possess a germ of truth, when he said on the question of indissolubility of marriage: 'With regard to the authority of Scripture I think those ingenious exercitations of the human mind on doubtful passages of Scripture rather tend to obscure their real meaning . . . and so to weaken and impair rather than to establish the just authority of Scripture' (see Chapter 11). One is content to believe that our Lord with his knowledge of human frailties and His kindness of

---

[1] *Report*, S.P.C.K., 1955, p. 8.

heart did not take a rigid view of marriage being totally indissoluble in particular cases.

However, the Christian fathers, as the ecclesiastical régime developed, accepted the principle laid down by Gratian, that a marriage once consummated was indissoluble, and if spouses parted neither could marry another. Nevertheless legal devices were invented to surmount the ecclesiastical veto by introducing an extremely wide system of nullity of marriage.

As pointed out in the 1955 Report of the Archbishops' Commission, already referred to, in the Middle Ages (and thereafter) the term *divortium* was used in two senses:

(a) *divortium a vinculo* in cases of nullity where the parties were declared never to have been married and therefore each was free to marry another;

(b) *divortium a mensa et thoro* in which in cases of adultery and cruelty a decree of separation was pronounced, but the marriage tie subsisted. This procedure has been carried down in the English matrimonial law.

Divorce, as we know it now, occurred under the Canon Law in the case of a Papal dissolution of an unconsummated marriage. In the thirteenth century A.D. Tancred set out the absolute bars rendering a marriage void as follows:

> *Error, conditio, cognatio, crimen, cultus disparitas, vis, ordo, ligamen, honestas, dissensus, et affinis, si clandestinus et impos, raptave sit mulier, loco nec reddita tuto. Haec facienda vetant connubiae, forta retractant.*

But the *Corpus Juris* included other grounds. The chief bars may be summarised as follows:

Mistaken identity of either party to the marriage; Holy Orders; consanguinity and affinity of relationship; adultery by spouse coupled with a promise to marry paramour or murder of other spouse; disparity of religion; bigamy; repudiation of betrothal; lack of consent; secret marriage; abduction and duress; impotence or insanity at the time of marriage; non-age.

All these grounds were called *impedimenta dirimenta,* and many of them have fallen into disuse in the Roman Canon Law. With such a multiplicity of grounds of nullity the medieval Church found in many cases a way out from the doctrine of indissolubility of marriage by making declarations of nullity, mainly in cases where money and influence came into play. The very wide rules of affinity during a period when communities were static were taken advantage of until the Lateran Council of 1215 got rid of most of such artifices and even reduced the impediment of consanguinity. This had been made to cover distant cousins, and even sponsors at baptism in the seventh century A.D., and the rules of affinity were even wider. If a man had a mistress her woman blood relations were reckoned as coming within affinity to the fourth degree, and even the relatives of godparents were at one time in the category of spiritual affinity. Thus when it suited a person to obtain a declaration of nullity the way was easy, subject to ecclesiastical court fees. Many of these legal fictions were abolished by the Council of Trent in the mid-sixteenth century.

For the development of law in England, based as it was largely on Roman principles, historians naturally turn to the books of Bracton *De Legibus et Consuetudinibus Angliae.* Henricus de Bratton (usually styled Bracton) (1216–72) was a learned lawyer who in the reign of Henry III, became a King's Judge and finished up as a clergyman of high degree. He said next to nothing about the law of marriage and nullity in his lengthy theses; but he accepted the view of Tancred[1] that in the law of Rome at that time if a couple took one another as man and wife in ignorance of any legal impediment, any children born after the union were legitimate. But the Lateran Council of 1215 put a stop to the doctrine of putative marriage by establishing the rule of marriage in church (*in facie ecclesiae*). Bracton clearly laid it down that under the Canon Law marriage was indissoluble during the lives of the spouses, despite the contrary principle found in the preamble to Henry VIII's Statute of Appeals in 1533. He asserted that if an ecclesiastical court excommunicated a person for any form of

[1] F. W. Maitland's note on 'Bracton and Tancred', Selden Society, 1895, p. 221.

contumacy, that person was debarred from suing for any civil wrong.

Another impediment much used from the time of Pope Innocent III (1192–1216) was such lack of consent as could be proved by the mental reservations of a spouse to true marriage. Under the Canon Law this method of nullity is still allowed, but this principle was not followed in England after the Reformation. In this country no agreement by the parties involving the frustration of one of the chief purposes of matrimony, or the mental reservation of one of the parties, ranks as a ground of nullity, once free consent to marry is given (see p. 18).

Ecclesiastical courts were set up to deal with cases of judicial separation, which operated in general to the detriment of married women. For instance, if a husband was a leper and infected his wife, it was not deemed cruelty and she had no remedy; and if she retired to a convent to escape from him she could be ordered to return to him. The Church tribunals also administered the law of nullity, whereby legal subterfuges opened up many forms of escape from the tie of marriage.

As stated by H. C. Lea in his *History of the Inquisition of Spain*[1]:

Society, so long as it was orthodox and docile, was allowed to wallow in all the wickedness which depravity might suggest. The supreme object of uniformity of faith was practically attained, and the moral condition of mankind was dismissed from consideration as of no importance . . . The world has probably never seen a society more vile than that of Europe in the fourteenth and fifteenth centuries.

Moreover, much profit accrued to the Church by reason of Papal dispensations to marry after sentences of nullity.

This period, disgraced by too many depraved Popes and Cardinals, greedy for temporal power and not overburdened with principles of personal morality, eventually gave way to more enlightened times. The Rev. William J. Doheny, in his encyclopaedic work on *Canonical Procedure in Matrimonial Cases*[2] said in the introduction:

[1] New edition, Cass, 1967, 4 vols.   [2] Bruce Publishing Co., Milwaukee, 1937.

16

Since the promulgation of the Code (*Corpus Juris Canonici*) the Holy See has observed that judges of matrimonial courts have experienced no little difficulty in adapting general principles to the individual cases appearing before ecclesiastical tribunals. In particular the Sacred Congregation of the Sacraments has been keenly cognisant of the dangers to which the sacrament of matrimony and the honour of the Church have been exposed, when unskilled judges are called upon to decide matters of such great moment. Another reason for assiduous care in deciding matrimonial cases is the insidious attack being made on the Church by the enemies of the Christian faith, which would fain represent her as preparing the way for divorce by casuistic devices; while, on the contrary, she merely decides the question of the validity or invalidity of a marriage as it actually existed at the very first moment of the matrimonial alliance ... Wherefore Bishops are invited to take cognisance of the expressed mind of the Holy See ... that specially young men, educated at least to the doctorate in Canon Law in Rome, should be properly instructed in court procedure and trained to decide cases correctly, especially in the Sacred Roman Rota, under the aegis of justice and truth.

The canon law treats the contract of marriage not only as creating status but also as a sacrament, which latter was preserved in the Reformed Church of England, as all who make their sacred vows in church may see from the Prayer Book. Under the Canon Law the only indissoluble marriage (apart from the principles of nullity) is a consummated marriage of people who have been baptised in the Roman Catholic Church. If such marriage has not been consummated it may be dissolved by Papal dispensation. On this ground Pope Alexander VI dissolved the marriage of his daughter Lucrezia Borgia on her asseveration that her marriage to Giovanni Sforza had not been consummated, and the latter's agreement that that was true. This pontiff left an infamous reputation in a very loose age, and died in 1492 of a dose of poison which he intended for someone else.

Strict rules have been laid down for the proof of non-consummation in cases where not only baptised spouses but also one or both of the spouses are not baptised within the Roman Church but invoke the Pauline privilege (1 Cor. 7: 12–15) in seeking divorce as distinguished from nullity.

The grounds of nullity in the Roman Canon Law have now been reduced to those in English law (see Chapter 12), plus celibacy of priests, non-age (under sixteen years in England) and defective intention and conditional consent to marry. This last mentioned impediment has been rejected in English ecclesiastical and civil law as tending to undermine the true principles of marriage. The Archbishops' Commission on the Law of Nullity said in its Report:

The principle would seem to hold good that the intention (of parties to a marriage) must be collected from the words of the rite which they employ and not from any private intentions which they may have . . . English law looks to the consent as expressed and will not allow the parties privately to derogate from their public professions.

Canon 1086 of the *Corpus Juris* states that the internal consent of the will (of a person at marriage) is presumed to correspond to the words or signs used in the celebration of marriage. If one or both of the parties exclude, by a positive act of the will, marriage itself or all right to the conjugal act or any essential property of marriage, the contract would be invalid. Simulation is never to be presumed but must always be proved.

A sentence of nullity was pronounced by the Roman Rota in 1911 when the woman petitioned and the man was proved to have gone through the form of marriage merely as a temporary union, with the motive of securing her fortune. In another case in 1915 a nullity was granted on proof that the man, an impostor and confirmed rogue, entered into marriage merely to gain his wife's fortune. In a third case in 1922 a woman in love with a man went through a form of marriage with another man to get away from home, promptly deserted her putative husband, who was granted a nullity on the ground of the woman's simulation. The archives of the Sacred Rota abound in such decisions, but cases of mental reservation without such surrounding facts are comparatively rare, such as the Marconi case (*Acta Apostolicae Sedis,* 1927) in which the famous pioneer of wireless telegraphy was granted a decree of nullity on the ground of a condition agreed between the spouses at the time of the marriage being contrary to its true nature. The cause célèbre of Consuela Vanderbilt and the Duke of Marlborough (*Acta Sedis,* 1926), in which the wife was granted a nullity, was based on a different ground, duress by her mother.

Though figures are not readily available, those for 1953 give an indication. According to *Le Monde* of Paris the tribunal had for trial that year 337 cases of nullity. Of those 200 concerned Italians and the rest applicants from other countries. The court decided 170 cases of which 76 resulted in sentences of nullity and the remainder in validity of marriage.

As regards the impediment of clandestinity in the Roman Canon Law governing nullity of marriage it is of some historical interest to refer to the so-called divorce by Napoleon of the Empress Josephine. He had married her in 1796 by a civil ceremony, invalid in the eyes of the Canon Law, but later the Pope refused to crown Napoleon until he went through a religious ceremony with Josephine conducted by Cardinal Fesch, but without witnesses. In 1807 Napoleon, having decided to marry Marie Louise, contrived to obtain a judgment of nullity from a French ecclesiastical tribunal on the ground of informality in the religious ceremony. Josephine did not appeal, so the nullity sentence was accepted by all and sundry, except the Sacred Rota (see Chapter 7, p. 67).

3 Divorce in England

From the sophisticated life of Rome and its dependencies let us turn to the conditions prevailing in what have been styled the barbarian lands in the north of Europe. When in the fifth and sixth centuries A.D. the Franks and the Goths invaded the Western Empire they did not obliterate Roman laws and usages. The Dark Ages doubtless obscured much learning and literature but many Teutonic tribes had already absorbed the notions of Roman civilisation. Charlemagne, who had sanctioned the Christian faith among his peoples, was crowned Emperor in Rome on Christmas Day A.D. 800 and though his empire soon crumbled the lasting influence of the Christian Church spread its sway under the Emperor Otto.

Large regions of Germany and Scandinavia, however, had never experienced Roman rule, so that when Britain, from which the Romans retired early in the fifth century, was invaded by various Teutonic and Danish tribes they brought with them their laws and customs, which as time went on were influenced by the Roman Christian law. St Augustine the monk (the lesser saint) introduced Christianity to King Ethelbert of Kent in A.D. 597, when the Saxons were almost supreme in southern England, and King Arthur in the west, with his magic sword Excalibur, was but a glorious tradition.

England was at this epoch a land of forests, rivers and lakes, traversed by the Roman roads. Roman culture with its ordered civilisation was decaying. Tribal chiefs lived in wooden houses and scattered settlements, and paganism still prevailed. It is no part of this book to attempt to describe the general laws and customs of the Celtic, Anglo-Saxon and Scandinavian settlers in this island, so well depicted by far more learned authors, only to deal with the marriage laws that prevailed here after the growth of Christianity.

With the advent of Christianity came the priests with their knowledge of law and clerical skill. King Ethelbert was the first of the English kings to reduce to writing the customary laws of the states. The Anglo-Saxon form of marriage was at first preceded by an agreement between the wouldbe husband and the bride's parents for *mund*, a generic term meaning the rights and duties of the wife. This included the equivalent of the Jewish dowry and was later replaced by a species of settlement on the bride. A priest officiated at the marriage ceremony. The wife owned her property.

Divorce could be obtained by mutual consent, as in the early Roman civil law, or by reason of the wife's adultery or desertion. But the Canon Law gradually developed in England as the Church increased its scope, with its principle of indissoluble marriage. But in 669 the Canons issued by Theodore, Archbishop of Canterbury, still permitted modifications such as freedom for a spouse to marry someone else after the other spouse had been in hopeless captivity for five years, or had been in desertion for the same period, though a woman whose husband had been condemned to slavery must wait a year before marrying again.

In a moving passage in his *Mediaeval Foundation of England* (Collins, 1966), Sir Arthur Bryant writes:

So it came about that in the seventh century England became a Christian land. From Canterbury Roman monks carried their missions into Wessex—the kingdom of the West Saxons—making Christians of the warrior farmers who had driven the Britons beyond Exe and the Severn. From Northumbria the disciples of Aidan took their message of faith and goodness to the peoples of Mercia. Though they only partly comprehended its revolutionary creed of love, humility and self-sacrifice, it came to them as a

C

wonderful revelation. It took the darkness out of their sad, fatalistic beliefs and offered them hope and purpose.

The *Ecclesiastical History of the English Nation* of the Venerable Bede (673–735) is a valuable source.[1] As in the case of the Roman upper classes and their slaves or freedmen, so in Anglo-Saxon times the background of the governing classes and the serfs cannot be ignored in relation to the laws of marriage and divorce. Those were mainly applicable to the governing classes. The laws of the kings of Wessex threw little light on the obligations of marriage. King Ine (A.D. 688–725) enacted: 'If anyone buys a wife and the marriage does not take place, the bride's guardian must return the bridal price and pay the bridegroom as much again.' Sir F. Pollock, treating of archaism in one of his learned *Essays in the Law*[2] pointed out that the formula 'With this ring I thee wed' was borrowed from the oldest Germanic laws, and was a vital condition of the contract. There was an elaborate system of surety and pledge.

For example, King Alfred (871–900) enacted that a betrothed young woman who committed fornication must pay the value of sixty shillings in livestock to the surety of the marriage, and if her 'wergeld' was six hundred shillings she must pay one hundred shillings. Adulterers were similarly penalised; and a husband might fight without being liable for reprisal, if he found another man with his wife within closed doors or under the same blanket, or with his sister or daughter or even his mother in the same circumstances. King Ethelbert (d. 616) enacted: 'If a man lie with the wife of another man he shall pay her husband his wergeld, and procure another wife for the husband with his own money.'

Thanks to the efforts of the monks and Christian pilgrims the new faith slowly grew among the tillers of the soil, the hewers of wood and drawers of water.

By the time of Edward the Confessor the Saxon dynasty was well in the saddle but a fresh epoch dawned with the advent of

---

[1] See article in *History Today*, June 1969, 'Bede of Jarrow, Father of English History', by Dr W. N. Bryant.
[2] Macmillan, 1922, p. 200.

William the Norman in 1066. Although the canon law of the Church had prevailed for long ere this the Norman conquest completed its supremacy, bringing to bear on England more learning and scholarship than before; serfs became freemen. The rule of indissolubility of marriage became general, borrowed from the Papal edicts, and this rule was never questioned until the Reformation, when the Tudor King Henry VIII sought to change the law to suit his own end (see Chapter 4).

At first the reign of the Norman kings made little difference to the lives of the common people. They went on ploughing their lands and cultivating arable and pastures, but their efforts were seriously handicapped by the royal forest laws, intended for the preservation of hunting grounds. Each parish had its church and priest, and the canon law of marriage prevailed. Some women who had been given in wedlock by their parents after the prevalent custom of buying and selling became nuns or anchorites to escape from their husbands. The Norman kings exercised certain rights in regard to the marriages of their vassals' womenkind, but Henry I ordained that licence to marry should not carry a fee, and should not be refused except in cases in which the wouldbe husband was hostile to the monarch. In 1096 Archbishop Lanfranc more or less completed the framework of ecclesiastical jurisdiction. For a valid marriage there must be a priest's benediction, and celibacy was ordained for the clergy. Later it was laid down that a valid marriage could be contracted by the declaration of the parties (*per verba de praesenti*).

Chaucer (1328–1400) who knew his world so well, in The Man of Law's Tale sang the lament of the Princess Constance who was destined for a distant sultan:

> *Women are born to thraldom and penance*
> *And to be under mannes governance.*[1]

Class differences pervaded domestic life, between the lord of the manor and his wife on the one hand, and the villein and his mate on the other. Again to quote Chaucer, in The Manciple's Tale:

[1] Trans. Tyrwhitt, Routledge, n.d.

Between a lady-wife of high degree
Dishonest of her body, if she be,
And some poor wench, no difference but this,
That if so be they both should go amiss,
That since the gentle woman ranks above
She therefore will be called his lady love
Whereas that other woman, being poor,
Will be referred to as his wench or whore.[1]

So the thraldom of the wife went on through the Plantagenet reigns. Girls who disliked their suitors, or loved some other man, were coerced into marriage willy-nilly, and even thrashed into submission. Love often won against temptation as depicted in Chaucer's Franklin's Tale:

The lordship husbands have upon their wives.
And to enhance the bliss of both their lives
He freely gave his promise as a knight
That he would never darken her delight
By exercising his authority
Against her will or showing jealousy,
But would obey in all with simple trust
As any lover of a lady must.[2]

By this time little social difference existed between the franklins and their tenants on the farms. Successful yeomen rose to the level of the gentry, like Clement Paston in the reign of Richard II, whose son William became a Judge.

In his *English Social History* (Longmans, 1942), Sir G. M. Trevelyan stated:

The peasants knew some of the sayings of Christ, and incidents from his life and from those of the saints, besides many Bible stories such as Adam and Eve, Noah's flood, Solomon's wives and wisdom, Jephthah and his daughter 'the which he loved passing well'. All these and much more with many strange embellishments he learned from 'pious chansons' and from the friars'

[1] Trans. Nevill Coghill, Penguin Classics, 1951.   [2] *Ibid.*

sensational and entertaining sermons. He never saw the Bible in English, and if he had he could not have read it. There was nothing in his own home, analogous to family prayers and Bible reading. But religion . . . surrounded his life. The crucifix was often before his eyes, and the story of the crucifixion in his mind.

But already a spirit of revolt was stirring against the exactions and the dominance of the Church, ruled to a great extent from Rome. What did William Langland, the poor man's poet, say in *Piers Plowman*:

> *Many chaplains are chaste, but where is their charity?*
> *There are no harder, hungrier men than men of Holy Church,*
> *None more avarous than they when they are set on high,*
> *Unkind to kinsmen and to all Christian souls*
> *They eat up their charity and grumble for more.*
> *Many parish priests are clean in body,*
> *But, encumbered with covertise they cannot drive it forth,*
> *So close hath avarice clasped them together.*
> *Avarice is no virtue. It is hell treachery*
> *It teaches the lay people ungenerously to give.*[1]

The Paston letters in the troubled times of the Wars of the Roses show how two love marriages in the family were contracted. In one case John Paston, a determined young man whose father was dead, won the affection of one Margery Brews, despite a difficulty over dowry, and made her his bride. In the other case Margery Paston obstinately adhered to her secret engagement to marry the estate bailiff, defying the veto of her family until they gave way. But there was an Agnes Paston who was brutally oppressed by her parents into submission.

On the other hand we read of the sad case of one Elizabeth Paston, a girl whom her mother tried to bully into marrying one Scrope, a fifty-year old widower. It is recorded that for three months she had been 'beaten once in the week or twice in one day, and her head broken in two or three places'.[2] Surviving these

---

[1] Trans. A. Burrell, Everyman's Library, 1912.
[2] H. S. Bennett, *The Pastons and Their England*, Cambridge University Press, 1960.

severities she was offered like a piece of property after some years to a marriage with one Poynings. Even in those days the lines of Tennyson in his fantastic but melodious medley of ancient and modern, *The Princess* would not have seemed false to most people:

Man for the field, woman for the hearth,
Man for the sword, and for the needle she.
Man with the head and woman with the heart:
All else confusion.

Among the peasantry what are now vulgarly styled shot-gun marriages often resulted in holy wedlock, perhaps free from the bridal price. But girls in higher society were carefully protected from importunate wooers. Moreover, the Paston letters paint a picture of young matrons faithfully performing their household duties, and organising the catering for their families, keeping accounts of expenditure, sewing and dressmaking. Nor were they by any means all the slaves of their husbands. Within certain limits the matrons dominated the menkind which is doubtless true in all ages.

Until the late nineteenth century the general lot of spinsters without means of their own was either to toil for their younger brothers or sisters or to find employment as ill-paid and little respected governesses. But in medieval times many of them were sent to nunneries, with due fees to those establishments. Education was spreading in the fifteenth century. More schools were founded. Latin was the written language of the governing classes, and the spoken words of the cultured, probably pro-nounced in the continental way rather than the anglicised form common in English schools in the nineteenth century. It was Caxton (1422–91) with his printing press who did much to bring back the beauty of the English language. All these developments helped to bring more gentle civilisation into married life. But the Canon Law still prevailed. Marriage was indissoluble save by nullity or death.

Superstition and belief in witchcraft and necromancy were widespread in England as in Europe. Fears of the devil and his evil doings prevailed for centuries later, and indeed black magic has a few votaries to this day. An odd sidelight on the crude and almost infantile belief in the ancient practice of putting needles in the small images of people whom their enemies wished to do away with has been extracted by Hugh Ross Williamson[1] in connection with Humphrey, Duke of Gloucester, onetime Regent to his nephew, Henry VI. As a boy George, later the ill-fated Duke of Clarence, found in a lumber room in Baynard's Castle on Thames-side, a faded wax image, which he showed to his brother, later Edward IV, who then told George about a *cause célèbre* of the century. The Duke of Gloucester had obtained a decree of nullity of marriage from his first wife and married his mistress, Eleanor Cobham. She was reputed to have ensnared him by means of magical potions, prepared by a notorious practitioner in necromancy, the Witch of Eye. The new Duchess was told by a renegade priest, Roger Bolingbroke, who dabbled in the Black Art, that she was destined to become Queen of England, on the death of Henry VI. These machinations came to light. Bolingbroke was hanged and quartered. The Witch of Eye died at the stake, and the Duchess was sentenced to life imprisonment, after doing penance by walking barefoot on three days through the streets, clad in a white sheet. The Duke is said to have been ignorant of his wife's action but shortly afterwards died in custody.

[1] In *The Butt of Malmsey*, Michael Joseph, 1967.

4 The Reformation

Catherine of Aragon

When we come to the Tudor dynasty already the growth of Lutheranism and the powers and abuses of the Church and the pontiff in Rome had led to discontent in England. The immense range of influence and patronage which Wolsey gathered into his hands under Henry VIII doubtless inspired that monarch to take action when the Cardinal fell into disgrace. The expropriation of the monasteries followed, sparked off by the prolonged contest between the Pope and the King over the so-called divorce of Catherine of Aragon, Henry VIII's first wife. Conflicts of jurisdiction between the ecclesiastical tribunals and the civil courts had occurred, and the King asserted the authority of the latter in their proper sphere.

Perhaps Marvin H. Albert, the American author, in his fascinating book *The Divorce* (Harrap, 1966), puts it too high when he writes in the preface:

It [the 'divorce'] influenced the course of world history more pointedly than the battle of Waterloo. Without it there might have been no Drake plundering the Spanish Main, no Invincible Armada, no Dutch or English colonisation of America. England might never have arisen from a third-rate power to the strongest nation on earth and Holland never have won its independence. Spain might not have declined, and the United States of America never have been born.

The sad story of Queen Catherine is worth retelling because it shows how the King, in order to take a new wife who might bear a son, heir to the throne, finally and fraudulently secured an edict of nullity of marriage. Moreover, in the prolonged and abortive negotiations with the Pope for a true sentence of nullity it became manifest that the canon law was set at nought through the King's desperation. The youngest child of the dominating Queen Isabella of Castile, Catherine was born in 1485. Like her mother she was short and stout, but never lacking in gentle grace. In those days when to be royal was to rule and make powerful alliances abroad, princes and princesses became betrothed at the will of their parents when they were mere boys and girls. Thus, for political reason, Catherine at the age of eleven was betrothed to Arthur, the elder son of Henry VII of England. She was about a year older than he. They were married by proxy two years later, and after much delay, due mainly to Henry VII's more ambitious schemes, she voyaged to England. After a tiring journey she sheltered for the night at a house known now as Cardinal's Wharf, Bankside, on the south side of the Thames.

A marriage ceremony took place at St Paul's Cathedral; she was then fifteen and a half years old, and met for the first time her boy husband's young brother Henry, aged ten. He was robust and sporting, Arthur sickly and retiring. Catherine was already a cultured girl, a fluent linguist, and adept in the musical accomplishments of those days. It is said that Henry VII forbade his son Arthur to consummate the marriage, and whether or not he obeyed the paternal order became a question of some legal importance in view of later developments. Arthur died in 1502 and the Princess of Wales with her retinue was doomed to a dull life, widowed and neglected, in poor circumstances. Her mother, Queen Isabella, in vain appealed to Henry VII, a miserly monarch, to give Catherine her due or send her back to Spain. The King had other plans, and Catherine's father, Ferdinand of Aragon, was either indifferent to her fate, or helpless.

Eventually Henry VII saw advantage in his son Henry marrying Catherine, and obtained Pope Clement's dispensation for the union, notwithstanding the canon law forbidding marriage with a brother's widow, but on the basis that the marriage had not been consummated. In the Bishop of Salisbury's palace in Fleet Street Prince Henry was formally betrothed to Catherine. Similar dispensations had been made by popes for royal alliances, as in the case of King Emmanuel of Portugal to wed the Infanta Maria after the death of her sister Isabella, the King's former wife. Early in the fifteenth century King Henry IV of Castile, having no heir by his Queen, was granted a papal dispensation to marry again, on the condition that if then he did not beget an heir he should re-marry his first wife.

It is said that Henry VII delayed the marriage for political reasons, but when he died in 1509 Henry VIII finally espoused Catherine, and she was crowned at Westminster Abbey. In 1516 Princess Mary was born. Other children were born, but did not live.

Henry VIII, as we know, was a despotic monarch, and longed for a male heir. He had his mistresses. His eldest son, Henry Fitzroy, later Duke of Richmond, born in 1519 of Elizabeth Blount, became Lord High Admiral. Anne Boleyn, niece of the Duke of Norfolk, came into Henry's life. His infatuation for her was intense. He named a ship of war after her. History would make us believe that there was a long period of frustration on her part. Be that as it may, Anne had no doubt from his protestations and love letters of his passion for her, 'Wishing myself to be in my sweetheart's arms whose pretty dubbies I trust shortly to caress.' And did not Anne declare the great love he bore her 'in the bottom of his stomach'.

A Pope, to placate no doubt the growing dislike of the King and the English people for the power of the Church, had given Henry VIII the title of 'Defender of the Faith'. Added to that was Henry's overweening craving for a son and heir. Marital intercourse had ceased between the royal spouses. Catherine and Mary were living a miserable existence, under the King's disgrace.

Wolsey at his master's behest had sounded Pope Clement VII with a view to getting rid of the King's marriage, but the Emperor Charles V was too powerful an adversary on his niece Catherine's behalf to overcome, and in 1527 the Pope was practically the Emperor's captive. With reluctance Wolsey gave some colour to the King's pretensions that his marriage to his deceased brother's widow was invalid in Canon Law, despite the papal dispensation. The argument seems to have been that the pontiff had no right to give his dispensation for Henry's marriage, and that therefore he had been living in sin with Catherine.

Another point was raised, which seems to have been ill-founded —that Catherine's marriage to Arthur had not been consummated and therefore it was not a true marriage in Canon Law. The obvious answer would seem to be that if it were not a valid marriage then Catherine was free to marry Henry VIII. Oh, no, said some ecclesiastical lawyers at Henry's behest: there was a pre-contract between Arthur and Catherine which precluded her marriage to Henry. Catherine always maintained that there had been no marital intercourse with Arthur, that she was a virgin when she married Henry, and this was duly reported to the Pope. Throughout, Henry VIII made a great display of his conscience and how the Almighty had deprived him of a son by Catherine as a punishment for his carnal sin. A boastful remark by Arthur to one of his associates just after the marriage in England, 'Last night I was in Spain', had been cited as evidence of consummation at the time of the papal dispensation.

Cruel pressure was brought to bear on Catherine, a woman of great integrity and fortitude, to agree to Henry's will. But she had the support of Charles V and the Pope was afraid to defy him and loath on religious and lawful grounds to decree a nullity. Nevertheless he sent his delegate, Cardinal Campeggio, to England after a long delay, to act as conciliator and, if necessary, as arbiter. Both the Cardinal and Wolsey pleaded time after time with Catherine to give way, on some occasions on their knees. She would not take vows of chastity, a canonical ground for nullity. Henry declined Cardinal Campeggio's suggestion that he and his wife should come together again, on the Pope's granting a fresh dispensation. Henry told her that his conscience forced him to take action and she must retire to a nunnery. She protested in vain. Once in desperation she cried out: 'I am no English woman but a born Spaniard.' The plot was public knowledge. She had general sympathy. The populace reviled Anne Boleyn. 'No Nan!' they cried out.

In June 1529 what purported to be a trial of the issue was opened at the Chapter House in Blackfriars, with Cardinals Campeggio and Wolsey as the tribunal and Henry in attendance. On her knees, but behaving with dignity and humility, Catherine appealed to the King for justice. Catherine said that she was a virgin when she married him, had been a true and obedient wife and borne him children. She said: 'It is a wonder to hear that new inventions are now invented against me that have never intended but honesty, and cause me to stand to the judgment of this new Court, wherein you may do me much wrong, if ye intend any cruelty . . . They cannot be but indifferent counsellors for my part which must be your subjects and dare not for your displeasure disobey your will and intent.'

She curtseyed to the King and left the court, and returned to Bridewell Palace. On the last day of the trial, towards the end of July, Cardinal Campeggio refused to pass sentence, and adjourned the sitting for two months. The King departed, consumed with anger, leaving his chief advocate Wolsey 'naked to my enemies'.

Cardinal Campeggio returned to Rome, having successfully avoided the King's displeasure. In his *Henry VIII* Shakespeare records in the mouth of the Duke of Suffolk that letters from Wolsey to the Pope entreating him to stay the judgment of divorce came to the eyes of the King. History records how soon afterwards Wolsey was deposed from all his offices and died in 1530, a broken man, before worse could befall him. Later Sir Thomas More, the Chancellor and theologian, also became a victim of Henry VIII's resentment over his brave refusal to accept the nullity of Catherine's marriage, and was beheaded for high treason in 1535. This was decreed by a special court of satellites of the King, headed by Thomas Cranmer, later the first Archbishop of Canterbury in the reformed church.

Catherine steadfastly refused to recognise the 'divorce', as it was called, and the validity of the King's marriage to Anne Boleyn. She told messengers from the King that if she confessed to their persuasions, strong inducements having been held out to her, she would confess to having been the King's harlot. Henry's ill treatment of Catherine and of her daughter Mary, who was declared illegitimate, are on record. The Pope excommunicated Henry and declared that the 'divorce' and Henry's marriage to Anne Boleyn were invalid. The latter's daughter Elizabeth was made Princess of Wales. The grim fate of Anne, who had failed to produce a living son, is well known. Archbishop Cranmer pronounced Anne never to have been the lawful Queen. In an attempt to justify this declaration, despite her much publicised coronation, the Archbishop convened an ecclesiastical court which purported to annul Anne's marriage on the grounds of the impediments of a pre-contract with the Earl of Northumberland and Henry VIII's affinity by reason of his previous intercourse with her sister.

In Shakespeare's treatment of this historical episode in *Henry VIII* he puts into the mouth of Suffolk:

> *Cranmer is returned in his opinions*
> *Which have satisfied the King for his divorce,*
> *Together with all famous colleges*
> *Almost in Christendom.*
> *Shortly, I believe, his second marriage*
> *Shall be published and her [Anne Boleyn's] coronation.*
> *Katherine no more shall be called Queen, but*
> *Princess dowager and widow to Prince Arthur.*

Henry VIII died in 1547, having had six wives, and Edward VI died after a short reign. Cranmer had short shrift from Catherine's daughter, the devout Roman Catholic Queen Mary, and perished at the stake in 1556. It may be said in Cranmer's favour that he consistently supported his sovereign in breaking the bond of Roman Mother Church and helped to compile the Book of Common Prayer.

Meanwhile Henry VIII and his parliaments had been busy passing laws which finally extinguished the suzerainty of the Church of Rome in England, leaving the King in practical control of the clergy and their livings. His Statute of Citations (1531–2,

33

23 Hen. VIII, c. 9) aimed at the abuses of procedure in the ecclesiastical courts, enacted that no manner of person should henceforth be cited or summoned or otherwise called to appear out of the diocese in which he dwelled.

More important was the statute (32 Hen. VIII, c. 38) since entitled the Marriage Act 1540, concerning the degrees of consanguinity, the terms of which, having regard to the King's personal record, make somewhat ironical reading, with its invocation of 'God's law'. In modernised language it reads:

Whereas heretofore the usurped power of the bishop of Rome hath always entangled and troubled the mere jurisdiction and legal power of this realm of England, and also unquieted much the subjects of the same by his usurped power in them as by making unlawful which by God's word is lawful, both in marriages and other things . . . and till now of late in our sovereign lord's time . . . have so continued the same, whereof some sparks be left which hereafter might kindle a greater fire, and so remaining, his power not to seem utterly extinct.

Many inconveniences have ensued and many more might follow: as where heretofore many persons, after long continuance in matrimony, without any allegation of either of the parties, or any other, at their marriage, why the same matrimony should not be good, just and lawful, and after the same matrimony solemnised and consummate by carnal knowledge, and also some time fruit of children ensued of the same marriage, hath nevertheless, by an unjust law of the bishop of Rome which is, that upon pretence of a former contract made and consummate by carnal copulation (for proof whereof two witnesses by that law were only required) been divorced and separate, contrary to God's law and to the true matrimony both solemnised in the face of the church, and consummate with bodily knowledge and confirmed also with the fruit of children had between them, clearly frustrate and dissolved, further clearly also, by reason of other prohibitions than God's law admitteth, for their lucre by that Court invented, the dispensations whereof they always reserved to themselves, as in kindred or affinity between cousins-german, and so to fourth degree,

carnal knowledge of the same kin, or affinity before in such outward degrees, which also were lawful and not prohibited by God's
law, and all because they would get money by it, and keep a
reputation for their usurped jurisdiction, whereby not only much
discord between lawful married persons hath contrary to God's
ordinance, arisen . . . and great damage of the innocent party
hath been procured, and many just marriages brought in doubt
and danger of undoing, and also many times undone, and lawful
heirs disinherited.

But . . . since freedom in them was given by God's law, which
ought to be most sure and certain, . . . not withstanding marriages
have been brought into such an uncertainty thereby, that no
marriage could be so surely knit and bounden, but it should lie in
either of the parties' power and arbiter, casting away the fear of
God, by means and compasses to prove a pre-contract, a kindred
or alliance, or a carnal knowledge to defect the same, and so
under the pretence of these allegations afore rehearsed to live
all the days of their lives in detestable adultery, to the utter destruction of their own souls and the provocation of the terrible wrath
of God upon the places where such abominations were suffered
and used.

After this long preamble it was enacted that marriage contracted
and solemnised in the face of the Church, and consummated with
bodily knowledge, or fruit of child, being had between the parties
so married, should be lawful and indissoluble,

notwithstanding any pre-contract of matrimony not consummate
with bodily knowledge which either of the persons so married or
both shall have made with any other person or persons before the
time of contracting that marriage . . . and that no reservation or
prohibition, God's law except, shall trouble or impeach any
marriage without the levitical degrees.

Finally the spiritual courts were forbidden to entertain any
process, plea or allegation contrary to the Act. But in 1548 the

Act 2 and 3 Edw. VI, *c.* 23 repealed the major part of the Act of 1540, enabling the ecclesiastical courts under the sovereign's authority to carry on much as before in regard to nullity of marriage. Thus the popular dislike of the papal predominance came to a climax through the personal ambition of a ruthless monarch.

5 The Urge for Divorce

Although the Marriage Act 1540 was rendered ineffective in the main within ten years of its passing, Henry VIII and his parliament abolished practically all the other powers of the Church of Rome over England. Peter's Pence and fees to the clergy went by the board. Among educated classes anticlericalism was widespread. Erasmus had consistently attacked sacerdotalism and the luxurious lives of the monks, 'gorging the carcase to the point of bursting', and expressed the utmost contempt for the preaching of the friars. So the stage was well set in public opinion for the dissolution of the monasteries, which enriched many Court favourites and founded the fortunes of noble families. Many of the enlightened clergy favoured this reform, and took advantage of the new law abolishing celibacy for priests. For many years past both bishops and parish priests had looked with suspicion and contempt on the ways of monks, who employed vast retinues of servants, described in Starkey's *England*[1] as 'idle abbeylubbers, apt to do nothing, but only to eat and drink'.

Thus the time was ripe for an improvement in the Church laws, and in 1552 the *Reformatio Legum Ecclesiasticarum* was formulated, having been originated by Henry VIII, who appointed a body of commissioners, and compiled under the aegis of Archbishop Cranmer. Herein was the germ of our later laws of divorce on the familiar grounds of adultery, desertion and cruelty, but it never became law. The Royal Commission on Divorce which

[1] Thomas Starkey, *England in the Reign of Henry VIII*, EETS, 2 parts, 1871–78.

reported in 1912 under the chairmanship of Lord Gorell, a former President of the Probate Division in England, considered the *Reformatio* in detail.

In a memorandum to the Commission the eminent jurist Sir John Macdonell pointed out that many of the reformers were of opinion that marriage ought to be regulated by the state; that almost all of them rejected the doctrine that marriage was a sacrament; and the majority held that marriage was dissoluble, though there had been great uncertainty, even in Luther's view, as to the causes for which it might be lawfully dissolved. Erasmus had admitted a wide variety of grounds of divorce. Beza in his sixteenth-century book *De Repudiis et Divortiis* limited the causes to adultery and desertion.

Sir John cited one of the numerous theses of the silver-tongued Puritan divine Henry Smith (who died in 1591) as follows:

Divorcement which is the end of marriage, and divideth them that were one flesh, as if the bodie and soul were parted asunder. But because all performe not wedlocke vowes, therefore He which appointed marriage hath appointed divorcement, taking our priviledge from us when we abuse it. As God hath ordained remedies for every disease so He hath ordained a remedie for the disease of marriage. The disease of marriage is adultery, and the medicine thereof is divorcement. Thus He which made marriage did not make it inseparable, for then marriage would be a servitude.

Sir John said that the *Reformatio* was a statement by eminent ecclesiastics and lawyers to be the law. No divorce was to be decreed except by an ecclesiastical court, and was to be permitted for adultery, contumacious desertion for two or three years, too long absence without news of the absentee, and in certain circumstances of persistent cruelty. Separation *a mensa et thoro* was to be abolished.

There was some evidence that for half a century marriage was held both by the Church and State to be dissoluble. The following passage from Strype's *Memorial,* Book II, ch 23 (seventeenth century) illustrates what happened:

The nation now became scandalous for the frequency of divorces, especially among the richer sort. Men would be divorced from their wives with whom they had lived many years, and by whom they had children, that they might satisfy their lusts with other women. . . . That which gave occasion also to these divorces was the covetousness of the nobility and gentry, who used often to marry their children when they were young boys and girls, that they might join land to land, possession to possession, neither learning, nor virtuous education, nor suitableness of temper and disposition regarded: and so, when the married persons came afterwards to be grown up, they disliked many times each other, and then separation and divorce and matching to others that better liked them followed, to the breach of espousals and the displeasure of God.

But in Foljambe's case (1601) the Star Chamber held on the declaration of Archbishop Whitgift that adultery was only a case for divorce *a mensa et thoro* (equivalent to our judicial separation). Nevertheless there are several cases in the old reports of the early seventeenth century when divorce *a vinculo* was decreed, and the case of *Foljambe* was not one for divorce, the dispute being about something quite different. The issue concerned a claim by one Rye, of Aston, Yorkshire, to an estate which had passed to his daughter after her husband, one Poaze, had died. She had gone through a form of marriage later with Hercules Foljambe (or Fuljambe) to whom she granted a lease of the estate for forty years. But it turned out that at the time of this marriage a former wife of Foljambe was still living. Foljambe's plea was that Mrs Poaze had induced him to marry her, with the knowledge that he had been granted an ecclesiastical sentence of divorce against his former wife on the ground of her adultery. Archbishop Whitgift held that this was only a divorce *a mensa et thoro,* and Foljambe's marriage to Mrs Poaze was a nullity.

In its Report (1912) the Royal Commission stated:

Whatever irregularities may have taken place in the times immediately following the Reformation, we find subsequently

39

recognition by all of the fact that without a private Act a valid marriage could not be dissolved . . . *Box's* case in 1701 appears to have been one of the first if not the first case where, without any special circumstances, the legislature granted a divorce *a vinculo* after sentence in the Arches Court.

In fact there had been earlier cases of decrees of divorce by private Act of Parliament on the ground of adultery (as will be seen in Chapter 7).

The somewhat summary reports of this case scarcely do justice to its[1] complications. Similar decisions were made in the case of *Stephens* v. *Totty* in the King's Bench a little later, and in *Powel* v. *Weeks,* affecting a legacy and dower respectively, to the effect that an ecclesiastical divorce was not *a vinculo*.

Followed the case of Sir John Stawell, a big estate owner in the west country. He sued his wife for divorce on the ground of adultery. Eventually the case came before the Archbishop's Court. Queen Elizabeth was petitioned to intervene and she appointed a Court of delegates. They found the wife's adultery and pronounced a sentence of divorce *a mensa et thoro* in 1565.

Seven years later Stawell wished to marry Frances Dyer, whose brother Edward was a Court favourite, and sought the permission of the Bishop of Bath and Wells to marry her. Archbishop Parker acceded to his request. They married, but his first wife then sued Stawell for restitution of conjugal rights and charged him with entering into a bigamous marriage. Apparently, from Sir Lewis Dibdin's thorough researches, these proceedings were adjourned *sine die*. Sir John died in 1603, having made a settlement to safeguard the children of his second marriage from being held to be illegitimate. His first wife took action to obtain a declaration recognising her as the wife of Sir John and her right of dower, and in 1605 she was successful in the Court of Common Pleas on the latter plea. It would seem also that the original sentence of divorce was held to be merely one of separation, according to the ecclesiastical law.

[1] Moo, p. 683; 3 Salkeld, p. 137; Noy, p. 100. See Sir Lewis Dibdin, *English Church Law and Divorce,* 1912.

Notable changes had occurred in the social and economic life of the country in early Tudor times, in a population of some four million souls. Unemployment was rife; usury was rampant, until in 1552 it was prohibited by statute; inflation, to use a term so common nowadays, was on its way. The confiscation of the monasteries was applauded by the people as a whole, but the destruction of many monastic libraries with their manuscripts was a cruel injury to learning and literature, although schools and hospitals developed after the Reformation. Agricultural production increased with the gradual merging of small peasant holdings into bigger farms. Lawyers prospered. Trevelyan in his *English Social History* says:

The road opened yet wider for the men of law in the exciting, litigious and rapacious times of Henry VIII and his children, when lawyers of an adventurous turn had unusual opportunities to serve the government, and receive a very full reward, especially when, as in the case of the Bacons and the Cecils, law was blended with courtiership and politics. Many of the lovely Tudor homes that still adorn the English landscape were paid for by money made in the Courts of Law.

The importance of this development lay in the increase in the jurisdiction of the common law courts and the gradual falling-off of the influence of the ecclesiastical courts, despite the latter's continuing monopoly of jurisdiction in matrimonial and probate matters.

This was the background of the Reformation period in England. Special privileges of the clergy such as immunity from civil actions and some crimes if they took sanctuary were swept away. Henry VIII discouraged the study of the canon law and encouraged the Civilians, a college of advocates which had already sprung into being earlier in the sixteenth century, comprising professors and doctors of law, and eventually settled in Doctors' Commons in Knightrider Street near St Paul's Cathedral. Entry as advocates was restricted to doctors of law at Oxford or Cambridge Universities who had been admitted by the Dean of the Arches, the supreme ecclesiastical court, under the authority of the Archbishop of Canterbury. These advocates practised both in the ecclesiastical and chancery courts, and in sundry other tribunals, including the Court of Admiralty. They advised in international private law and diplomatic affairs. They alone as time went on were qualified to become judges of the ecclesiastical courts and the Court of Admiralty. It was mainly due to them that legal literature was disseminated in the universities and elsewhere. The solicitors who instructed the advocates in this fraternity were styled proctors. It was not until the Judicature Acts of the 1870s that this body was abolished, when for convenience their functions were transferred to the Probate, Divorce and Admiralty Division of the Supreme Court.

The opposition of the common lawyers and prohibitive decisions by the common law courts gradually wore away the influence of the Civilians except in the ecclesiastical jurisdiction over matrimonial and probate causes. Towards the end of Queen Elizabeth's reign all the advocates in Doctor's Commons were laymen. In 1575 the Crown gave the College the right of importing wine free of duty for consumption by the members.

The Roman canon law lasted longer in Scotland, then a separate kingdom, than after the Reformation in England. Somewhat earlier Margaret Tudor, widow of James IV, had married the Earl of Angus but obtained a sentence of nullity and married Lord Methven, but again, discontented with her lot, procured a further sentence of nullity against him on the ground of the impediment of affinity, Lord Methven being a very remote cousin of Lord Angus.

Again in Scotland the impediment of pre-contract survived the Reformation, but the Scots thus early borrowed from Calvin and the Geneva theologians the system whereby divorce could be pronounced on the grounds of adultery and malicious desertion, the ecclesiastical jurisdiction giving way for this purpose to a civil tribunal. Lord Salvesen (later a Scottish Lord of Appeal) said in his evidence to the Royal Commission on Divorce in 1910 as to the introduction of adultery as a cause for divorce without statute after the Reformation: 'The Roman Catholic Church treated marriage as a sacrament.' When the Reformation came there was a change of opinion, at all events in Scotland, and marriage was no longer treated as a sacrament. Therefore it came to be regarded from the point of view of a contract which might be dissolved as far as that could be done consistently with public morality, and at once, apparently, divorce for adultery was introduced. An Act of 1573 recognised this as an existing institution. Lord Salvesen added that this Act was introduced really for the benefit of an Earl of Argyll who wished to get rid of his wife. The Earl had married the half-sister of Mary Queen of Scots. She had deserted him and he could not induce her to return. The Act of 1573 was passed, Lord Salvesen thought, especially to meet this case. He quoted the preamble to the Act to the effect that a spouse since the Christian religion was established could always divorce the other after four years' malicious desertion. Certain preliminaries such as a disobeyed ecclesiastical admonition were abolished by the Scottish Conjugal Rights Act of 1861.

Incidentally, it may be mentioned as a light touch, the addiction of Scottish lawyers to the Roman law in other respects was such that if a Latin term could be found to express a familiar object or legal principle they were eager to seize on it. Thus it is recorded that where a case concerned the sale of some bustles, an article of female adornment much in fashion in the nineteenth century, the advocate confessed himself at a loss to cite an equivalent Latin term, at which the judge observed: *'Quite easy, aliquid superbum.'*

Little occurred in the reign of Queen Elizabeth to vary the law of indissoluble marriage. Our merchant venturers expanded English influence overseas, life became easier for the people, with abounding prosperity for many. Spain's threat ended with the Armada. London's population rose to 200,000. But child marriage still went on, with the system of wardship in the upper classes.

6 The Seventeenth Century

With the dawn of the seventeenth century, and James VI of Scotland enthroned in 1603 as King of England, London was not only the great trading centre but also the largest port in the kingdom, with Bristol next. The rich became richer, the many poor poorer, as inflation continued to rear its ugly head. Poor relief created in Elizabethan law was only too necessary. Most of the clergy were still Roman Catholics, and many were poor and ill-educated. Calvinism emphasised the accuracy of the Bible text. Divorce *a vinculo* not having been enacted, the remedy of nullity on tenuous grounds became the remedy, although statistics are not available owing to the absence of consistorial court records. The new translation of the Bible in 1611 enriched our literature. Trans-Atlantic colonisation began.

If one turns to Shakespeare, most of whose plays were published in the reign of James I, there is scarcely any allusion to divorce as it is now understood. Some references are made to the canon law of nullity so often styled divorce in those times. Thus in *The Winter's Tale* (Act IV, sc. 3) Prince Florizel of Bohemia says to his disguised father Polixenes: 'Mark our contract' (with Perdita), and his father retorts: 'Mark your divorce, young Sir!' And in *Measure for Measure*, a play depicting the corruption of society, Claudio is shown to have seduced his betrothed Juliet before a formal union had been completed, then a crime carrying with it possibly the death penalty.

The strong canonical bar of consanguinity was instanced in

44

Hamlet, by reason of Queen Gertrude's marriage to her slain husband's brother-in-law Claudius. In such an act (Act III, sc. 4) we find Hamlet's words about adultery:

> *. . . makes marriage vows*
> *As false as dicers' oaths. O! such a deed*
> *As from the body of contraction plucks*
> *The very soul, and sweet religion makes*
> *A rhapsody of words.*

In *All's Well that Ends Well* (Act V, sc. 3) Helena claims Bertram with the words:

> *If it appear not plain, and prove untrue,*
> *Deadly divorce step between me and you.*

Shakespeare, of course, used as we do the term divorce in its non-legal sense as meaning 'divide' or 'alienate', as in *Richard II* (Act III, sc. 1), when Bolingbroke (Henry IV) told his ill-fated captives:

> *You have in manner with your sinful house*
> *Made a divorce between his Queen and him.*

Also in Act V, sc. 1, where Northumberland says to Richard: 'Take leave and part, for you must part forthwith', and Richard exclaims:

> *Doubly divorced! Bad men, you violate*
> *A twofold marriage; 'twixt my crown and me,*
> *And then, betwixt me and my married wife.*

In *Henry VI*, Pt. 3 (Act I, sc. I) Queen Margaret reviles the King for his surrender to York (Edward IV) and Warwick, saying:

> *Thou prefer'st thy life before thine honour:*
> *And seeing thou doest, I here divorce myself*
> *Both from thy table, Henry, and thy bed . . .*

having no doubt in her mind the legal process of divorce *a mensa et thoro*.

In *The Comedy of Errors* (Act I, sc. I) we find the merchant Aegion lamenting the loss of his wife by shipwreck: 'this unjust divorce of us'; but in *Othello* (Act IV, sc. 2) there is Desdemona's cry to Iago: 'Though he [Othello] do shake me off To beggarly divorcement', clearly a suggestion of a nullity suit.

A case decided by a special commission of bishops appointed by James I was that of Frances Howard, who at the age of thirteen was married to the then Earl of Essex, aged fourteen years. They never came together, and Frances was eventually courted by Robert Carr, later Earl of Somerset. She refused to accept her husband, and was granted a decree of nullity by the commission and married Carr. Both were later disgraced because of their complicity in the murder of Sir Thomas Overbury. It is true that James I introduced the law of bigamy, but otherwise the laws of marriage and divorce remained unchanged, and this position continued throughout the reign of Charles I and under Cromwell's Commonwealth.

If we look at the code of ecclesiastical canons enacted under James I in 1603, Canon 105 provided that no sentence of divorce might be pronounced merely on the confession of the parties, and it was clear that such sentence referred only to divorce *a mensa et thoro* or to a decree of nullity of marriage. But even these remedies were not to be lightly allowed, because the canon proclaimed:

Forasmuch as matrimonial causes have been always reckoned and reputed among the weightiest, and therefore require the greater caution, when they come to be handled and debated in judgement, especially in cases wherein matrimony, having been in the church duly solemnized, . . . we do straitly charge and enjoin that . . . good circumspection and advice be used, and that the truth may be sifted out.

Canon 107 provided:

46

That the parties so separated shall live chastely and continently; neither shall during each other's life contract matrimony with any other person.

In 1713 Edmund Gibson, later Bishop of London, produced his famous commentary on the canons, rubrics, and articles of the Church reinforcing the fact that judicial separation and decrees of nullity were the only remedies.

It is notable how personal situations have on occasion induced individuals to promote laws calculated to ease or advantage their own or someone else's difficulties, as so fully illustrated by Henry VIII in the 'divorce' of Catherine of Aragon. John Milton (1608–74) was another such case. In 1643 he married a girl of seventeen, Mary Powell. He was on the Puritan side, she belonged to a Royalist family. After a month she left him and rejoined her mother. Later she offered to return to Milton. He refused and in his indignation put his prolific pen to the work of urging a law of divorce. In a number of published theses he proposed by a sweeping reform of the marriage law to 'wipe away ten thousand tears out of the life of men'. He wanted to marry another woman, but when in 1645 his wife on her knees implored him to take her back he relented and did so, and they had four children—hardly an irretrieval breakdown of marriage.

Nevertheless Milton's eloquent advocacy of a law of divorce, however inspired, influenced many minds. In his preface to *The Doctrine and Discipline of Divorce* (1643–44) he wrote:

What thing more instituted to the solace and delight of man than marriage? And yet the misinterpreting of some scripture directed mainly against the abuses of the law for divorce given by Moses hath changed the blessing of matrimony not seldom into a familiar and coinhabiting mischief; at least into a drooping and disconsolate household captivity without refuge or redemption.

He criticised the 'uncharitable' canon law and said 'Marriage was thought so experimental that no adultery or desertion could dissolve'. He paid a tribute to the 'wisest and gravest Christian

47

emperors whose statutes and edicts were far more easy and relenting, and also to Grotius for his more enlightened view'. He added: 'Not that licence and levity and unconsented breach of faith should however be countenanced but that some conscionable and tender pity might be had of those who have unwarily made themselves the bondmen of a luckless and helpless matrimony.'

Milton wrote: 'Christ neither did nor could abrogate the law of divorce but only reproved the abuse thereof . . . Fornication in the ancient sense was not confined to actual copulation . . . The law forbidding divorce never attains to any good end, but rather multiplies evil.' He invoked the example of Henry VIII in putting away his wife Catherine thus:

Parliament and the clergy of England consented that Henry VIII might put away his queen Anne of Cleves, whom he could not like after he had been wedded half a year: unless it were that they made a necessity of that which might have been a virtue in them to do; for ever the freedom and eminence of man's creation gives him to be a law in this matter to himself, being the head of the other sex which was made for him; whom therefore though he ought not to injure, yet neither should he be found to retain in society, to his own overthrow, nor to hear any judge therein but himself . . .

Henry VIII, finding just reason in his conscience to forego his brother's wife [Catherine of Aragon] after many indignities of being deluded, and made a boy of by those his two cardinal judges, was constrained at last, for want of other proof, that she had been carnally known by Prince Arthur, [reduced] even to uncover the nakedness of that virtuous lady, and to recite openly the obscene evidence of his brother's chamberlain.

Yet it pleased God to make him see all the tyranny of Rome by discovering this which they exercised over divorce, and to make him the beginner of a reformation to this whole kingdom, by first asserting into his familiary power the right of just divorce.

In Chapter III Milton spoke of 'The ignorance and iniquity of canon law providing for the right of the body in marriage, but nothing for the wrongs and grievances of the mind'; in Chapter IV

48

he wrote: 'Marriage as our Saviour bids was not properly the remedy of lust but the fulfilling of conjugal love and helpfulness.' He wrote in Chapter VI: 'Marriage is more broke by a grievous continuance than by a needful divorce . . . Where love cannot be, there can be left of wedlock nothing but the husk of an outside matrimony, as undelightful and unpleasing to God as any other kind of hypocrisy . . . It is a less breach of wedlock to part in wise and quiet consent betimes than to foil and profane that mystery of joy and union in a polluting sadness and perpetual distemper'; and in Chapter IX he added: 'Adultery is not the greatest breach of matrimony; there may be other violations as great.' Powerful words, prophetic of the divorce law brought about by the Matrimonial Causes Act, 1857, and extending Acts since for the relief of hapless marriages.

It is not the purpose of this book to trace by chapter and verse throughout the seventeenth century all the influences and teachings that enlightened, or during some periods, darkened the minds of the English. The Protestant Church became well established, strengthened by the Thirty-Nine Articles and the writings of Hooker, Sir Thomas Browne in his *Religio Medici*, John Donne in his reformed days, Jeremy Taylor and many others.

Despite the conflicts between Charles I and his parliaments and in the Civil War between Cavalier and Roundhead, social life was not uprooted, not even in the Commonwealth of Cromwell. There was no such social chaos as overtook the French in their revolution (see Chapter 8). The temporary eclipse of many of the nobility and high gentry ceased on the Restoration of Charles II. Although we know that astute king was foremost in the moral corruption that prevailed in his court, but yet won great popularity as the Merrie Monarch or 'Old Rowley', except during the violent anti-Catholic years, there is little evidence that social life in general changed for the worse. The Restoration plays depicted the loose life of high society, and the frank revelations of Samuel Pepys in his diary pointed to the moral depravity of family life. But marriages were celebrated as usual in church with the prayer book vows. The population reached over 5 million. Married women were still treated as subservient to their husbands, although in many cases no doubt they ruled their mates by superior craft and intelligence. Nevertheless wives had no property rights in law. Pepys's entry in his Diary (19 Dec. 1662), 'My wife, poor wretch, is troubled with her lonely life', revealed the average man's point of view. But marriage was the ambition of most girls, to govern their households in preference to the tutelage of their parents. Yet such marriages were usually arranged by their parents, whether they liked their future partners or not. So it went on for a hundred years or more, though runaway marriages at Gretna Green and other places were not unusual, either based on mutual affection between the spouses or achieved by fortune-hunters at the expense of young heiresses.

Apart from the few doubtful cases of divorce which occurred rom time to time as a result of the abortive *Reformatio Legum Ecclesiasticarum*, no such process was possible until Parliament took a hand and permitted private acts of divorce.

7 Private Acts of Divorce

As early as 1546 Parliament (37 Hen. VIII, c. 30) ignored the ecclesiastical law and enacted that a woman was validly married to a second husband though her first husband, having disappeared for a long time, was still alive. Sir Ralph Sadler in 1534 married Elena, the wife of Matthew Barr who was believed to be dead. Barr, however, came on the scene again, and Parliament was constrained to enact in 1546 that the children born of the union between Elena and Sadler were legitimate; and if Barr obtained a decree of divorce *a mensa et thoro* on the ground of her adultery with Sadler she would become the legal wife of Sadler—a somewhat illogical reasoning and a topsyturvy arrangement, which, however, rendered the marriage with Sadler valid, with such rights as she might possess to property. This position for a deserted wife was not remedied until the Matrimonial Causes Act, 1937, section 8, permitted the court to presume the death of an absent spouse, subject to certain safeguards, and to grant a decree of divorce. If, however, the absentee reappears the decree has to be revoked, but the wife retains her remedy on a fresh petition based on desertion.

In the case of the Marquess of Northampton, brother of Henry VIII's sixth wife Catherine Parr, Parliament again intervened to render an invalid marriage valid, despite the ecclesiastical law. The Marquess obtained a divorce *a mensa et thoro* in 1542 from the ecclesiastical court against his first wife on the ground of adultery. He obtained an Act (34 and 35 Hen. VIII, c. 39) illegitimating the children of his wife. Next he went through a form of marriage with another woman, preferring not to await the decision of Archbishop Cranmer's Commission of delegates, appointed to consider whether in law he could do so or not; though eventually the delegates decided in his favour. At last in 1551 he contrived to obtain an Act which validated his marriage to the second wife, the Canon Law thus being overruled in his case. In Queen Mary's reign this Act was repealed. This repealing statute, however, did not expressly revoke the decision of the delegates who had found the second marriage valid. Their opinion reflected the contemporary notion that absolute divorce was justified in cases of adultery or desertion.

Whether or not John Manners, Lord Roos, later the Earl of Rutland, was encouraged by the precedent of Lord Northampton, about a century later he introduced a Bill in Parliament for sanction to marry again, having obtained a valid divorce *a mensa et thoro* against his wife on the ground of her adultery. The Bill was passed in the House of Lords by a majority of only two votes, most of the Bishops expressing their opposition to it. The Act did not purport to change the ecclesiastical law but only, as was stated by one of the peers, to create a dispensation in the particular case.

It is recorded by that sound historian Bishop Burnet, who played an important part in the restoration of Charles II to the throne, that this Divorce Act encouraged the King, moved by the Duke of Buckingham and other intriguers in his Court, to contemplate bringing in a divorce Bill against the Queen (Catherine of Braganza). She had failed to bear the King a living heir. The pretended grounds would have been, says the Bishop, that she was barren by a natural cause and had a certain secret defect in her person. A Bill accordingly was drafted but the King relented, and it was dropped. More is known nowadays about Charles II's relations with his Portuguese wife, and it would seem that he had a greater regard for her wellbeing, once she had become reconciled to his extramarital amours, than he has been given credit for.

Dr A. L. Rowse points out that Lord Roos's case caused a tremendous scandal but the political importance of it was greater, for the Whigs intended it as a precedent for a divorce by Charles II and the provision of a Protestant succession. Leading members spoke with much ardour and learning in the canon and civil law. Sir Winston Churchill, M.P. (father of the Duke of Marlborough), made a legal point which bore against the divorce: he was in the minority. So far as the King was concerned all were fooled: as a secret Catholic he had no intention of marrying again.[1]

There was even a more glaring case of parliamentary interference in the law in favour of the earl of Macclesfield in 1697. He put forward a Bill for the annulment of his marriage with a daughter of the Earl of Peterborough although he had not even obtained a sentence of judicial separation. An Act was passed accordingly.

Certain similarities were shown in the case of the Duke of Norfolk. In a criminal conversation action against Sir John Germayne on the ground of the latter's adultery with the Duchess, the Duke was awarded 100 marks damages. That was in 1692. The Duchess was not a party to this action. The Duke failed to obtain a separation order against his wife, but proceeded to bring in a Bill before the House of Lords for the dissolution of his marriage, and by a private Act in 1700 the marriage was annulled. It was put on the ground of the Duchess's adultery and also her failure to bear him an heir to the title and his property, and the Act enabled the Duke to marry again as if his wife were dead, she being excluded from all honours and benefits to which she would have otherwise been entitled.

The Duchess had answered the Bill by demanding more precise particulars of the charges of adultery, which she denied, pointing out that the offences were alleged to have been committed more than six years before the Duke presented his Bill. She said that she and the Duke lived in France together for some years from 1685 after which he returned to England 'in great passion of love, with tears in his eyes', and promised her an allowance of £400 a year, over and above moneys from a marriage settlement. When she returned to England in 1688 she sued him for alimony, the Duke having failed to pay her in full the £400 a year. In that action he did not charge her with adultery. She was awarded

---

[1] *The Early Churchills*, Macmillan, 1956.

E

53

£1,500 a year. She refused to join with him in the sale of certain estates, to which refusal she attributed the Duke's present charges; and she countercharged him with a course of adultery for the last ten years. 'I am not guilty of defiling my husband's bed', she declared.

That was her evidence. However, the report of the case shows that their lordships were satisfied on the evidence of witnesses that the Duchess had committed adultery in 1685. Yet the House of Lords threw out the Duke's Bill twice, in 1691 and 1692.

The Duke again petitioned the House of Lords in 1699, and on that Bill, according to the report, conclusive evidence was given of a course of adultery between the Duchess and Sir John Germayne until 1699. Some of their lordships demurred to passing the Bill without a previous sentence of separation by the ecclesiastical court but in fact the Bill was approved, subject to provisions for the Duchess being made. She afterwards married Sir John. Although in form the marriage was annulled rather than dissolved the case created a precedent for rich and influential men who under the ecclesiastical laws could not obtain an absolute divorce from their wives, or obtain a sentence of nullity from the ecclesiastical court because no ground could be proved.

Next comes Mr Copley's case in 1749. A sentence of separation having been pronounced by the Bishop of London in the Consistorial Court on the ground of Mrs Copley's adultery, the sentence was affirmed on appeal by the Court of Arches. Mr Copley presented a Bill for divorce which was duly passed. He had already been awarded damages against the adulterer in an action for criminal conversation and indecent familiarities.

In 1755 Captain Moreau's divorce Bill was rejected. The marriage took place in 1737. Two years later the husband went abroad, leaving his wife and child in financial straits. She wrote appeals to him in vain. He was away for ten years. Mrs Moreau lived with one Mr Smedley as man and wife for five or six years. The London Consistory Court had granted the husband a separation, but the House of Lords was satisfied that this decision was procured by collusion.

In all 317 private Acts of Divorce were passed until the Matrimonial Causes Act 1857 altered the system, and only four of these were in favour of married women. Many of them were of no general interest, though early cases showed a failure to obtain a previous sentence of the ecclesiastical courts. In 1769 the Duke of Grafton obtained an Act divorcing his wife on the ground of her adultery. Many Bills were rejected.

In 1736 Lady Foley petitioned for an Act of Divorce, having appealed from the sentence of the Consistory Court against her to the Court of Arches. That appeal was still pending and the House rejected the Bill till it was determined. The question whether a married woman could apply for a private Act was apparently not debated, but, as will be seen, this question was considered in later cases in the House of Lords.

In 1798 the House of Lords imposed a standing order to regularise this sort of proceeding. It was laid down that as preliminaries a husband must obtain a sentence of separation by an ecclesiastical court (untainted by collusion) and bring an action for criminal conversation against the wife's paramour, and the offending person should not be free to marry the adulterer. The whole cost of these proceedings would not be less than £1,000, a very large sum in those days.

In 1799 Admiral Sir Hyde Parker, famous in naval history, especially for his order at the battle of Copenhagen, to which Nelson applied his blind eye, petitioned the House of Lords for a divorce on the ground of his wife's adultery, and procured an Act accordingly, with a proviso declaring any of her children born between 1 May 1794 and 1 January 1797, when the Admiral was on naval service abroad, to be bastards.

In 1801 one Mr Cope's Bill was rejected on the ground of his own failure to protect his wife. In the same year the House of Lords on an Act of Divorce in the case of a Mr Taylor rejected an amendment that the guilty wife be forbidden to marry her paramour; and the case of Mrs Addison followed, in which the wife succeeded in obtaining an Act dissolving her marriage on the ground of her husband's adultery with her sister. The latter was the wife of a Dr Campbell who had been awarded £5,000 damages against Mr Addision in a criminal conversation action. Mrs

Addision had previously obtained a separation in the ecclesiastical court.

The question whether a wife could avail herself of this procedure caused a conflict of opinion in the House of Lords. Lord Eldon, the Lord Chancellor, though influenced by an eloquent speech by Lord Thurlow in favour of the divorce, said that adultery committed by a husband and that committed by a wife were widely different in their consequences. A wife's adultery might impose a spurious issue upon the husband, whereas no such injustice could result to the wife from the adultery of her husband. Samuel Johnson had expressed a similar view when he said: 'The difference between adultery by a husband and adultery by a wife is boundless.' But in those days methods of contraception were little known and rarely used.

The Duke of Clarence (later William IV) whose progeny by Mrs Jordan, the actress, were so well cared for later by Queen Adelaide, opposed the Bill on the ground of Mrs Addison's sex.

In 1805 a Mrs Teush petitioned the House of Lords for an Act of Divorce, on the ground of her husband's adultery and his brutal conduct to her. She obtained a sentence of divorce from the ecclesiastical court. Again Lord Eldon opposed the Bill, which was rejected by seven votes to three. Later the husband became domiciled in Scotland, where his wife obtained an absolute divorce, according to Scottish law. In 1831, however, a Mrs Turton was granted an Act of Divorce unopposed on the ground of her husband's adultery with her sister, mainly because of the affinity.

In the later case of Mrs Moffat in 1832, Lord Eldon revised his opinion, saying that he saw no reason why a woman was not as much entitled to sue for divorce as a man. Mrs Moffat had already been granted a sentence of divorce by the ecclesiastical court. But Lord Brougham, the Lord Chancellor, opposed the Bill on the somewhat strange reasoning that any man who desired to get rid of his wife had only to keep a mistress and to desert his wife, thereby driving her to obtain an Act of Divorce, and his purpose was served. In fact the Bill was rejected by sixteen votes to nine.

The case of Miss Turner in 1827 differed from an ordinary Divorce Bill in that it concerned the abduction and fraudulent marriage of a girl of fifteen over the Scottish border. Her abductors were convicted and sent to prison. An Act of Divorce *a vinculo* was passed unopposed, despite the fact that in law Miss Turner could have obtained a decree of divorce in Scotland.

The last case reported by McQueen of a woman's obtaining an Act of Divorce was in 1840. Mrs Battersby had the misfortune to marry a man who infected her with an 'infamous disease', and thereafter committed adultery and entered into a bigamous marriage, for which latter offence he was sentenced to transportation.

Few of the many other private Acts of Divorce call for comment. A considerable number of these Bills were rejected. In the case of Lord Cloncurry in 1811, his wife committed adultery with Sir John Piers. A duel followed between the two men, the result of which is not reported. It does not appear that Lord Cloncurry had obtained an ecclesiastical decree or sued Piers in a criminal conversation action, but the Act was passed.

In 1814 a Mr Dundas succeeded in his Divorce Bill on the ground of his wife's adultery with Lord Semple, having been granted an ecclesiastical decree of divorce. Lord Glerawley having been granted £1,500 damages against his wife's paramour was granted an Act of Divorce in 1821. From the case of Sir William Wiseman in 1824 for divorce on the ground of his wife's adultery with a midshipman in Jamaica it is seen that there was some demur on the part of their lordships because of doubt about the admissibility of the wife's confession to a witness, who was not before the House but had given his evidence in the ecclesiastical court. But the Bill was passed. In Lord Lismore's case in 1826 the question was raised whether the House could depart from the general rule that where there had been a separation between spouses, as in this case, no absolute divorce could be allowed. But the Bill passed on evidence of Lady Lismore's violence to her husband, who had been awarded damages against her paramour.

In these proceedings the House of Lords usually, but not invariably, required the filing of the ecclesiastical court's sentence of separation and also the depositions in that tribunal, and the Standing orders of the House in 1798 made clear this practice. But the House assumed the right of hearing witnesses itself when it deemed fit.

The procedure for a sentence of separation in the ecclesiastical courts required the citation of the person accused in the latter's diocese. The party cited could appear in person or by his proctor from Doctor's Commons. The charges were contained in what was called the Libel, in general, and allegations in particular. Elaborate regulations provided for pleas and counterpleas. Evidence was received upon deposition before examiners of the court. The case was then heard publicly in court, except that cases of nullity were heard *in camera*. Where the issue proved was desertion the court ordered restitution of conjugal rights, with certain pains and penalties for non-compliance. The cost of these proceedings varied between £100 and £500 according to the circumstances, although a longdrawnout case, with a possible appeal to the Court of Arches, might cost far more. Thus the procedure existed only for rich people.

Incidentally, there is not to be found in the many works on the English ecclesiastical courts any mention of a *Defensor Vinculi* (Defender of the Marriage Bond). Yet until 1857 the canon law of Rome was followed theoretically by the ecclesiastical tribunals in England in matrimonial causes. In the Roman courts under Art. 15 of the *Corpus Juris* the Bishop appointed a *Defensor Vinculi* to attend the trial, whose duty it was to uphold the validity of the marriage impeached (Art. 70). The proceedings were a nullity if he were not present, and his function was to examine the evidence, and if he thought fit, to appeal against a sentence of nullity or judicial separation. This advocate still performs his duties in Roman Catholic courts in England, and one can only assume that in the English ecclesiastical courts since the Reformation they had his equivalent, whether in the person of the judge or some other representative. Yet neither in the learned works of Oughton's *Ordo Judiciorum* (1728–38), Lyndwood, or Conset does one find any reference to a *Defensor Vinculi* in the English ecclesiastical courts after the Reformation.

In the House of Lords private Acts of Parliament many references are found to Bills rejected on the grounds of collusive deception of the court, connivance at adultery, condonation or recrimination by an accused wife. Moreover, when the ecclesiastical jurisdiction and procedure were abolished by the Matrimonial Causes Act 1857, except in regard to judicial separation and nullity, the Queen's Proctor was called upon to intervene, on cause shown, in those very matters (see Chapter 11).

The scrupulous care exercised by the ecclesiastical courts in trying cases was well illustrated in the suit brought by a nobleman in 1741–2 for a separation, as recorded in the archives of the Court of Arches. The procedure is detailed, and the incidents of adultery detailed without any reticence. The wife was accused of permitting a named lord 'to use her with great freedom and familiarity after a lewd and wanton manner'. It was alleged that on one occasion her hair 'was much tumbled'; Lord Tallbot's breeches being then unbuttoned; on another occasion of their embracing in a lewd and wanton manner, inducing her to exclaim: 'You make me extremely hot'; on another occasion in a wood Lord Tallbot 'getting from between her legs with his breeches down and her petticoats up which exposed her nakedness so plain that [the witness] saw her naked thigh'. The wife's answer was to recriminate with a charge of impotence against her husband.

Such implicit evidence of adultery, however, is not usually available, because as that great judge Lord Stowell said in *Williams* v. *Williams* (1 Hag. Con. 299): 'Direct evidence of the fact of adultery is not required, as it would render relief almost impracticable but there must be such proximate circumstances proved as in their own nature and tendency satisfy the legal conviction of the court that the criminal act has been committed.'

The action of criminal conversation (which in legal abbreviation was familiarly known as *crim. con.*) was brought by a husband against an alleged paramour of his wife, which latter, however, was not made a party. The charge had to be proved against the alleged adulterer, and damages awarded according to principles more or less carried on nowadays in a similar claim for damages against a co-respondent in a divorce suit (see Chapter 11).

59

But, although the *crim. con.* action had to be brought, even if it were unsuccessful or merely nominal damages were awarded, the House of Lords deemed itself free to deal with the Bill for divorce, paying proper regard to all the circumstances disclosed by the evidence.

8 The Eighteenth Century

The French Revolution

Social life so far as marriage and divorce were concerned continued in the England of the eighteenth century much as in the seventeenth. Conditions were fortunate for the aristocracy in general and the rich, and deplorable according to modern standards among the poor. In 1714 the population, owing to a high death rate, was under six million mainly in the rural south. Drunkenness and gambling were rife in all classes, together with cock-fighting and horse-racing. Improved education, however, led to a more general circulation of newspapers and pamphlets. John Wesley, at one time dubbed 'Pope John', spread his beneficent influence. In art and literature Dr Johnson, Robert Burns and Reynolds were supreme. But on the whole the lot of women was unchanged. They were still regarded as inferior, subject to the will of the father, and when they married, often as the result of financial bargains, to that of their husbands. Child marriages still continued among the monied classes for the enrichment of the opulent. Thus towards the end of the seventeenth century a grandson of the Duke of Bedford, aged fourteen, had married a girl of thirteen connected with the controllers of the fast-growing East India Company.

Trevelyan quotes from Lady Mary Wortley Montagu, who stood out from her epoch as an independent character of exceptional culture, as condemning certain local squires for being insensible to other pleasures than the bottle and the chase; 'The poor female part of the family were seldom permitted a coach, their lords and masters having no occasion for such a machine, as their mornings are spent among the hounds and their nights with as beastly companions—with what liquor they can get.' This, however, is not a true overall picture of the country gentry in Queen Anne's reign, most of whom seem to have led useful lives, looking after their families, administering their estates and serving as magistrates.

The evil of clandestine and illegal marriages spread widely. Unscrupulous and sham parsons made a business of performing the ceremony, in any convenient building. Young heirs and heiresses often fell victim to fortune-hunters, and imprudent passions stimulated the traffic. Lecky in his *History of England in the Eighteenth Century* (1788–90), stated that when ships came in and the sailors flocked on shore to spend their pay in drink and on prostitutes, from two to three hundred such marriages took place within a week. He recorded among the more notable cases of clandestine marriage those of the Duke of Hamilton with Miss Gunning, the Duke of Kingston with Miss Chudleigh, and Henry Fox with a daughter of the Duke of Richmond; and he pointed to the miserable case of the poet Charles Churchill, whose marriage at the age of seventeen cast a blight on his life, but yet in his bitterness did not deter him from this tribute:

> *Woman! By fate the quickest spur decreed,*
> *The fairest, best reward of every deed,*
> *Which bears the stamp of honour.*

The abuses of clandestine marriages at last became such a great scandal that Parliament took a hand. In 1753 Lord Hardwicke's Act 'for the better preventing of Clandestine Marriages' was passed. This measure stiffened the procedure of marriage by requiring the ceremony before a clergyman in an Anglican church, before witnesses and on due notice. Any infraction of the law made the offender liable to criminal penalties. Lord Hardwicke's Act was repealed by the Marriage Act 1823, which elaborated the rules and regulations of marriage. Later came the Marriage Act 1836, permitting civil marriages in register offices. The position is now set out in the code of law contained in the Marriage Act 1949.

Inasmuch as the laws regarding illegitimacy have been the subject of special legislation in England in recent years, it is not irrelevant to mention that bastardy was frequent in the eighteenth century, thousands of children abandoned in the streets, a public evil alleviated to some extent by the growth of hospitals and the endeavours of charitable institutions. The population was about $5\frac{1}{2}$ million at the beginning of Queen Anne's reign; in 1801 it had increased to 9 million, and in the next decade to $10\frac{1}{2}$ million. In London in 1800 it was 670,000, rising, after the industrial revolution, to 1,270,000.

Nevertheless there developed a much better life in rural communities, owing to the growing prosperity of the farmers and the middle classes, with their more solid houses, especially in the wool districts. Perhaps Wordsworth used poetic licence to portray the peaceful lives of the countrymen, but his pictures of the glories of the landscapes he knew so well were true to life in those days. In the villages rustic existence was almost cut off from the hectic life of London and the industrial towns which were rapidly extending their boundaries. The squire reigned supreme, but on the whole peace and quietude prevailed, and sturdy families were raised, mostly free from the squalors of town life.

But with the beginning of the industrial revolution came immigration to the manufacturing districts, and a consequent change in rural life, as the exodus increased. In *Eighteenth Century Society* (Penguin Books, 1950), Dr J. H. Plumb shows us the other side of the coin in London and industrial towns. No sanitary system existed. Cesspools and refuse thrown into the streets abounded. The Thames served as a sewer. The poor lived in hovels. Disease took its vast toll. Only one child in four survived. Yet by the end of the century public health improved. The birthrate in London at last exceeded the death rate.

It is not irrelevant to mention how in this age of aristocratic dominance the arts were cultivated, the literature of the eighteenth century was rich and plentiful in its output, the Empire spread throughout the world, despite the loss of the American colonies.

But beneath the surface a new spirit arose, the beginnings of democracy. Peterloo and the rick-burnings, the Gordon riots, the evils of factory life and child labour were only some symptoms of the unrest which led to the advent of Tom Paine (1737–1809), author of *The Rights of Man* as a revolutionary, and Richard Cobbett the reformer. Yet high life under Whig or Tory continued unchanged, marriages of convenience were still frequent, and in general, with a few notable exceptions, women were still treated as the inferior sex, though mistresses of their own households, with plentiful cheap servants.

In the 1780s Revolution in France brought in its train a period of chaos in social conditions, with marriage a farce and divorce for the asking. In the days of the Frankish monarchs the marriage and divorce laws of the early Roman emperors prevailed in their dominions, until the canon law of Rome was substituted and prevailed until the revolution. In 1792 marriage became a civil contract with a civil ceremony and obligatory registration. But divorce could be had by mutual consent or even at the will of either husband or wife, and judicial separation became a thing of the past. A local tribunal registered the fact of a divorce without inquiry. Unfettered by law divorce became rampant and society was plunged into an orgy of sexual chaos. Few of the French writers on the Revolution deal with this aspect of it, being chiefly concerned with its political developments.

M. Jean Robriquet, a former keeper of the Musée Carnavalet, author of *La Révolution de 1789* (1938),[1] researched more deeply into this subject. He pointed out that under this régime no priest officiated or attended at a marriage. A notice posted up at the town hall announced the coming 'marriage of A. and B. who intend to live together in lawful marriage and who today will present themselves at the municipal offices to reiterate the present promise and to have their intentions legalised by the law of the state'. The notices surmounted by a Phrygian cap set out the new laws of marriage and divorce. Such notices appeared at the mairie on the Place de la Grève, notorious for public executions and the

[1] English edition as *Daily Life in the French Revolution,* trans. James Kirkup, Weidenfeld & Nicolson, 1964.

grim machinery of the guillotine. The couple replied 'Yes' when asked the traditional questions, and thus became man and wife. So casual was the operation that as many as twenty marriages took place together with a chorus of 'Yeses'. The civil functionary in his tricoloured sash declared them married. Yet up to that time in all classes marriage had been celebrated with due solemnity in the presence of the priest. In small townships and villages the whole community had turned out rejoicingly for a wedding, with decorated church, the bride in white and a wreath of orange blossom, a more promising future for happy matrimony. Until the end of the *ancien régime* the indissolubility of marriage as laid down by the canon law was the rule. The Duke of Orleans, whose efforts for popular acclaim are well known, supported the intro-duction of divorce, and in 1792, on the motion of one Aubert Dubayet, the new law was adopted by the Legislative Assembly.

There was a contemporary diptych, which amused Anatole France, with the caption 'Republican Marriage and Republican Divorce'. In the first panel a municipal official is depicted greeting a couple about to marry. The groom in an English dresscoat holds the hand of the bride, with a plain fichu round her shoulders, wearing a bonnet with strings. Members of the family are in attendance to sign the contract. In the background is a huge statue of Hymen, the cherubic god of marriage, with his veil of flowers and flaming bridal torch in his hand. The second panel shows the same couple, with the wife in a fashionable bonnet, exchanging bitter words and turning their backs on each other. Members of the families are there to sign the divorce. Hymen's torch has been extinguished and the flower-chain broken.

Incompatibility was the usual pretext. With such a loose law, married life became no more than a series of passing fancies, and oddly enough, wives were no less eager to change partners than the husbands. 'They changed their name and their status', wrote Robriquet, 'as they changed frocks and hats.' One of the most singular features, he adds, was that many couples thus separated came together again: just as easily as the law facilitated divorce it rejoined estranged couples. This might have been as a result of the political cry at the height of the Revolution—'France needs children'. Processions of women marched through the streets with banners inscribed: 'Citoyennes, give children to the Patrie! Their happiness is assured.' Chamberpots bore similar devices. There was an exhibit at the Musée Carnavalet of a bedpan for a woman in labour, with an inscription: 'This is the moment for a little baby.'

Naturally the Church opposed this return to paganism, which was not general throughout France. Religious feeling was disgusted. Yet even at Notre Dame a fête took place with an actress on the altar as the goddess of reason. The Merveilleuses and the Incroyables with their transparent dresses contributed to the spate of immorality. The calendar changed in 1793, no more sabbaths or saints' days, but seven days of national festival, together with a day for a Fête des Epoux. A revolutionary, the Marquis de Fontvieille, who helped to kill fellow aristocrats at Lyons, divorced his wife and married a marquise, also divorced, one of the Merveilleuses. It was the period between August 1792 and August 1794 during which this social chaos was at its worst.

The advent of Bonaparte as the First Consul heralded a return to a more orderly system in respect of divorce. The Code Civil of 1803 retained divorce by mutual consent, provided that the parents or remoter ancestors gave their consent. The procedure in court was stiffened. There had to be four appearances, with judicial recommendations for conciliation, before a divorce was pronounced. This costly process would delay a divorce for two years. Better arrangements provided for the maintenance of children and the division of the spouses' property. In the case of a divorce by mutual consent the parties could not enter into a fresh marriage for three years, and, moreover, after twenty years of marriage, or after a wife had reached the age of forty-five, divorce was forbidden. An adulterous wife could not marry her paramour, and whether guilty or innocent she had to wait for six months after a divorce before she could marry another man. Judicial separation was revived, subject to the right of converting into divorce after three years' separation. But a wife guilty of adultery could be granted a divorce, only with her husband's consent. The ground of incompatibility in contested cases was abolished. Adultery, cruelty and conviction for serious crime became grounds for divorce.

Napoleon with his wiser advisers realised the importance of the integrity of the family to the nation, but upheld the husband as the governing head. The matrimonial articles were more or less reproduced in the Code Napoleon of 1807. Nevertheless Napoleon as Emperor paid no obedience to his own Code when with the purpose of begetting an heir to his throne he divorced Josephine to marry the eighteen-year-old Princess Marie Louise. With some heartburnings he made his decision after his successful Wagram campaign. He summoned a family gathering for 10 December 1809 and broke the news, to the horror of his wife. But she had to acquiesce, with Malmaison and other estates and a settlement of £150,000 a year as a sop, and the right to retain the empty title of Empress.

Bonaparte's civil marriage to her had been followed by a secret religious marriage, but without the appropriate curé and witnesses. Cardinal Fesch, his uncle, protested, but on a papal dispensation he had officiated. Before the divorce Napoleon made a declaration that he had not given his full consent to the religious marriage but only agreed to a futile ceremony to satisfy Josephine and the Pope.

On his fiat the marriage, after a *senatus-consultum,* was dissolved, with the approbation of the French ecclesiastical and civil authorities, but against the refusal of Pope Pius to recognise the divorce, or nullity as it was described. Napoleon's marriage to Marie Louise in 1810 was by proxy, followed by a gorgeous ceremony in Paris. Josephine died just before Napoleon's first abdication in 1814.

Napoleon was on a visit to Flushing after the marriage when he saw among those gathered to receive him a Papal representative. In one of his angry outbursts he expressed his resentment against the Papal excommunication, exclaiming: 'Render to Caesar the things that are Caesar's. I am Caesar to whom God has committed the sceptre and the sword.' He lived to regret his marriage to Marie Louise, and in exile referred to it as 'an abyss covered with flowers'.

One of the phases of Napoleon's later career was his vision of imperial glory. Already as self-made Emperor in 1804 he had done his best to revive in his court the pomp and protocol of the *ancien régime*. Six years later he set the seal on his ambition to enter into the centuries-old dynasty of Habsburg by marrying Marie Louise, daughter of His Royal and Apostolic Majesty the Austrian Emperor. However much Napoleon tried to manifest the dignity and splendour of his court, even to the extent of employing four queens—of his own creation—as train-bearers for Marie Louise at her coronation, he failed in his purpose. It was all pinchbeck to foreign observers.

Nevertheless he seems to have instilled into his brothers and sisters a feeling of family pride in their sense of royal precedence, which prevailed among them long after St Helena. With Napoleon's mother, Madame Mère, exercising an almost autocratic sway over the numerous branches, most of the Bonapartes affected an attitude of ultra-respectability in their private lives in exile, anxious to avoid any breath of scandal. This development was notably illustrated in the little known case of nullity of marriage brought by Christine, a daughter of Prince Lucien, Napoleon's brother. It is only a sidelight on the history of the Bonaparte family, subsequent to Napoleon's death, but very many letters from almost every member of his family reveal their mixed feelings over the affair of Lucien's daughter.

In 1818 in Rome she married according to Catholic rites Count Arvid Posse, later Chamberlain to the King of Sweden (Bernadotte) Posse, a very unsatisfactory husband in many ways, moreover, was impotent. On that ground she obtained, despite legal difficulties and after long delay, a sentence of nullity from the Swedish Royal Tribunal in 1828, following a personal appeal by Prince Lucien to his friend of old days, Bernadotte. Full particulars of the Count's impediment were contained in the medical report.

Meanwhile Christine had fallen in love with Lord Dudley Coutts Stuart, son of the first Marquess of Bute, a frequent visitor to Rome, and he with her. She told him the sad story of her life with Count Arvid, whom she had left soon after the union. On a report, which proved erroneous, that he had died, they went through a secret marriage in church before a priest in 1824. When this came to the knowledge of Madame Mère and other members of the Bonaparte family it caused great perturbation among them, because in fact Count Arvid was still alive. Napoleon's mother and her brother Cardinal Fesch especially viewed with horror the notion of a granddaughter of hers living in sin. The numerous letters from most of Napoleon's brothers and sisters and their progeny about family matters included sympathy from some for Christine and Lord Dudley in their plight. He for his part at great expense, including a very large douceur to Count Arvid, set on foot Christine's proceedings for nullity, which reached their finale when the Papal Seal was affixed to the document endorsing the Swedish decree of nullity.[1] Apparently the Couple went through a second ceremony of marriage in Florence, and honour was satisfied. Later they lived in England.

In 1816 on the restoration of the Bourbon monarchy divorce was abolished and the canon law revived. But the Republican Code Civil restored civil divorce, except by mutual consent, and provided for a separation after a period of delay to be followed by divorce.

Balzac (1799–1850), who in his *Comédie Humaine* revealed a deep insight into human virtues and frailties, as a man of the world, dealt with the physiology of marriage in detail. In his semicynical style he termed marriage as a necessary institution to maintain the fabric of society but contrary to the laws of nature. He said little about divorce, in his age prohibited by the canon law, except that he regarded it as an admirable palliative to the evils of marriage. Fidelity, he said, was impossible, at least for a man. He questioned whether adultery caused more evils than marriage procured good, and criticised the article in the civil code which enacted penalties against an adulterous wife but did not punish a husband unless he installed his concubine in his home, with freedom to consort with her elsewhere.

With a considerable knowledge of the history of marriage and divorce in Europe from the earliest times, he referred his readers to Sanchez's twelve volumes *De Matrimonio* for deep study, and permitted himself a mixture of aphorisms, wise or wide of the

---

[1] Harrowby Papers, Vol. 24, in the Record Office.

mark, without, however, developing what he deemed to be a reasonable law of divorce.

The grounds of divorce under the existing French Code Civil are adultery, desertion, cruelty (included in the comprehensive term *sévices*, which covers grave insults or habitual drunkenness) unjustifiable refusal of conjugal rights; sentences of imprisonment for serious offences; and three years' separation.

9 Royal Marriages

Mrs Fitzherbert and Queen Caroline

It was not until some of the princes of the Hanoverian dynasty entered into marriages contrary to the will of the Sovereign that the Royal Marriages Act (12 Geo. III, c. 11) was passed in 1772 to restrict their free choice in future. That Act in its preamble said: 'Being sensible that marriages in the royal family are of the highest importance to the State', an oblique allusion to the succession to the throne when memories of the Jacobite risings were still alive. The Act forbade the contracting of such marriages and extended to the annulment of them, in violation of its provisions. It was enacted that no descendant of the body of George II, under the age of twenty-five years, except the issue of princesses marrying into foreign families, could marry without the consent of the Sovereign under the Great Seal. Such marriage was void *ab initio*, and everyone assisting in such marriage was liable to severe penalties. Descendants of George II above the age of twenty-five years might marry without the sovereign's consent, within twelve months of giving notice of such intention to the Privy Council, unless meanwhile both Houses of Parliament formally disapprove. This law has been applied to remoter descendants of George II and is still in force.

The clandestine marriages of William Henry, Duke of Gloucester, to the Dowager Countess of Waldegrave in 1766, and Henry Frederick, Duke of Cumberland, a brother of George III, to Mrs Anne Horton instigated the Act, but apparently in neither case was there an annulment. The Royal Marriages Act came into question in the Sussex Peerage case in 1844 (Clark and Finelly's *Reports*, vol. XI, 85). Prince Augustus Frederick, Duke of Sussex, sixth son of George III, in 1793 married Lady Augusta Murray, daughter of the Earl of Dunmore, in Rome, according to the rites of the Church of England. A more regular marriage between the parties followed in England. After the Duke's death in 1843 his only son claimed the peerage, and a question as to the validity of the marriage was referred to the House of Lords Committee for Privileges. The point was raised whether the Royal Marriages Act could be said to apply to a marriage abroad. The lengthy argument of the petitioner's counsel raised some doubts of the scope of the Act, but he submitted that as the marriage was valid in Rome it must be treated, apart from the Royal Marriages Act, as valid in England. It was held that under the Royal Marriages Act the marriage, in fact celebrated in due form, was invalid, and therefore the claim of the Duke's son failed.

The Sovereign may marry whom he or she wills. The Act of 1772 does not affect the Sovereign. In the Declaration of Abdication Act 1936 (1 Edw. VIII. c. 31) it was provided that the Act of 1772 should not apply to Edward VIII (the Duke of Windsor) nor to his issue, if any, or the descendants of that issue.

This Act loomed sinister in the passion of George Prince of Wales, heir to George III, for Maria Fitzherbert, twice widowed, a Roman Catholic. A handsome, cultured and versatile Prince, in 1784 he fell in love with this young widow, six years older than he. She was of good family and not attuned to the free-and-easy habits of the Prince's companions. She fled abroad to avoid his overtures, but his devotion persisted to the point of promising her marriage. A ceremony was secretly celebrated at her house, before two male relatives of hers, on 5 December 1785, despite the prohibition of the Royal Marriages Act and the Act of Succession. Under the latter statute such a marriage—to a Roman Catholic—forfeited the Prince's succession to the throne, and rendered the officiating Anglican clergyman, the Rev. Robert Burt, liable to pains and penalties. There were moments when the Prince declared to friends his intention publicly to avow the marriage, and abandon the succession to the throne, but wordly wisdom prevailed and the secret was confined to very few. The Prince allowed the denial to be made in Parliament that he had married Mrs Fitzherbert. They lived together as man and wife. She ceased to attend Court circles. They set up a home at Brighton where the Prince was extending the Pavilion. The public decreed her to be the Prince's mistress and the heroine of a lovers' romance. Lines in a popular ballad about them read:

I'd Crown resign to call her mine,
Sweet Lass of Richmond Hill.

In one of his caricatures Gillray made bold to portray the couple as 'Wife and no Wife'.

As time went on the Prince of Wales's unlimited extravagances involved him in heavy debts. Though Mrs Fitzherbert was the most devoted of partners it was scarcely surprising that his way-ward habits at times exhausted her patience. Under the influence of other ladies and Court circles he broke with her in 1794, a prelude to his marriage to Princess Caroline of Brunswick in the following year. Mrs Fitzherbert went into retirement on an allowance of £3,000 a year. There soon came a time when the Prince of Wales craved to return to his old love, and from 1796 he was making ardent overtures to her. In her heart and mind she was his wife, bound by the holy sacrament of marriage. After receiving a Papal Brief that as a matter of canon law she was entitled to regard herself as his lawful wife, and to rejoin him, a reconciliation took place in 1800, with a breakfast to their friends at her house in Tilney Street. They lived together at Brighton for eight years. Then the Prince left her again, mainly for political reasons. From then on Mrs Fitzherbert remained in dignified retirement, respected by and retaining the affection of nearly all the members of the royal family. The Prince Regent came to the throne on George III's death in 1820, and on George IV's death in 1830, his successor, the Duke of Clarence (William IV) ordered that Mrs Fitzherbert should be allowed to wear widow's weeds and to use the royal liveries. She died in 1837.

When George IV died, round his neck hung a miniature of

Mrs Fitzherbert. But the actual fact of her marriage to the Prince of Wales was still kept a secret, with the connivance of the Duke of Wellington and other statesmen. This suppression may have been due either to avoiding further royal scandal or for fear of dynastic trouble in the future, arising from a current rumour that she had given birth to two sons by the Prince of Wales. There is no extant evidence of the rumoured births, and in a statement written by Mrs Fitzherbert in 1836 she proclaimed that her union with the Prince was without issue. Proof of their marriage was not disclosed until early in the twentieth century when certain documents, published with the royal assent, put it beyond doubt. And so we come to the tragedy of the Prince's marriage to Caroline and his subsequent Divorce Bill after he succeeded to the throne, a proceeding which excited the anger of the populace and is so fully described by Roger Fulford in *The Trial of Queen Caroline*.[1]

On 8 April 1795, the Prince had been constrained to marry Princess Caroline, five years his junior. It was not a love match. The Princess, judging from her portrait, was by no means unbecoming, though she did not suit the Prince's taste. She soon became aware of his close association with Lady Jersey. The Princess was imprudent in her talk, and often behaved like a hoyden. She hurt the feelings of the Prince for the woman he really loved, Mrs Fitzherbert, by calling her 'fat, fair and forty', and later never hesitated to utter malicious quips at his expense such as that she had only committed adultery once, 'with the husband of Mrs Fitzherbert'. He treated her abominably. She was the daughter of Charles, Duke of Brunswick, a distinguished general on the Continent and the eldest sister of George III. Caroline was said to be lacking in decorum and notable for indiscretions, which grew into strange eccentricity. The only child of the marriage was the ill-fated Princess Charlotte who was born in January 1796.

The Prince found his wife unattractive physically and an open estrangement followed the birth of Charlotte. There was keen mutual dislike between husband and wife, and her neglected

[1] Roger Fulford, *The Trial of Queen Caroline*, Batsford, 1967.

condition gave a spur to her eccentricities and indiscreet friendships. In 1806 an important Commission was appointed to investigate her conduct. The Commissioners after hearing much evidence acquitted her of any immorality. Unfortunately she allied herself with the political party inimical to her husband, thus adding to his hatred of her. In 1814 she departed for the Continent, and in the course of her travels aroused great scandal by her associations with her Italian equerry Pergami and others. While she was wandering over Europe in a fantastic progress from city to city the Prince Regent used his influence not only to prevent her from being received in foreign courts but also to spy on her movements and conduct.

In 1818 the Prince Regent appointed another Commission to inquire into Caroline's conduct abroad, and after hearing Italian witnesses that Commission concluded that she had committed adultery with Pergami. On the death of George III the Princess returned to England to claim her rights as Queen. But George IV was intent on getting rid of his lawful spouse, and initiated a Bill for Pains and Penalties, on the model of a Bill of Attainder on the ground of her alleged adultery with one Bartoleommeo Pergami, who had soldiered in the Napoleonic wars and was first employed in the Princess's retinue as a valet-courier. In the Bill they were accused of a 'licentious, disgraceful and adulterous intercourse', and it was proposed that Caroline be deprived of the title as Queen, and that her marriage be wholly dissolved and annulled.

When this became known a storm of popular sentiment favoured the cause of the Queen, matched by an outburst of abuse of the King. Scurrilous cartoons of the King circulated widespread; a Cruickshank cartoon shows the Queen on her terrace being cheered by a group of ladies and gentlemen the latter waving their hats. Mobs collected outside her residence in London, cheering her wildly. George IV was not a popular monarch. Loyal addresses to the Queen reached her from all classes.

The proceedings began in the House of Lords, and if that chamber had passed the Bill it would still have been debated in the House of Commons. Judges were empanelled to give their advice if sought by the peers, all of whom were summoned to attend, but many managed to stay away. At that time the House was much smaller than it is today, and temporary galleries were improvised to accommodate an exceptionally large assembly of peers and officials.

The trial began on 17 August 1820. The Queen, then staying at a house in St. James's Square, drove to the House of Lords in a state carriage, drawn by six bay horses, with the King's livery. Cheering crowds sped her on the way. Lord Chancellor Eldon presided on the Woolsack. The Queen wore black sarsenet, in mourning attire for the recent death of the Duchess of York. Henry Brougham, as attorney-general to the Queen, demurred to the Bill on principle, as not within the jurisdiction. Thomas Denman, the Queen's solicitor-general, followed in eloquent terms. He said that the charge of adultery turned on the allegations of 'some suborned wretch from among the perjured abject pack, dragged by bribes from among the dregs of society in those countries which the Queen had visited'. He urged that the Duke of York (then heir to the throne) was guilty of all that was imputed to the Queen and much more. He referred to the possibility that she herself might inherit the throne because of her own descent from George II.[1] The King's attorney-general, Sir Robert Gifford, and his solicitor-general (the future Lord Chancellor Lyndhurst) urged the propriety of the proceedings as the only method of dealing with the charges. Other speeches followed and the Queen's demurrer was rejected.

Dealing with the charges against the Queen and Pergami the attorney-general said that at Naples in 1814 Pergami took a room adjoining the Queen's. She gave a masked ball to Murat, King of Naples, and dressed up as a Neapolitan peasant, a Turkish peasant, and as 'the Genius of History', the last in an indelicate costume, and Pergami helped to dress her. Her intimacy with Pergami and members of his family continued in Italy and Switzerland, in Tunisia and Greece, in 1815–16. When travelling in Syria the Queen slept in a tent, and Pergami was seen emerging from it in a state of undress. While travelling in Germany in 1817 some of her clothing was seen in Pergami's bed. On the journey

[1] Fulford, *op. cit.*

back from Austria to Italy Pergami alone was her carriage companion.

Had the evidence in support of this and other incidents of the Queen's intimacy put forward by the attorney-general come up to proof the trial might have taken a different course. But in subsequent sittings the evidence wore thin. Theodore Majoichi, employed in the Queen's household at Naples in 1815, recounted the sleeping arrangements of the Queen and Pergami, and her visits for a few minutes to his room when he lay there with an injured leg in an accident. He said he made the beds and observed that Pergami's bed had not always been occupied. Further evidence was given concerning the intimacy between the Queen and Pergami, such as the latter having a bottle in which to make water when he was travelling in the Queen's carriage. Majoichi was cross-examined by Brougham, who made mincemeat of him, thoroughly discrediting him as a suborned witness for the King.

Gaetano Paturzo, a Neopolitan, described how aboard a ship in the Mediterranean he had seen the Queen and Pergami walking arm-in-arm on deck, and the Queen sitting in his lap, with her arm round his neck. He suggested that the sleeping arrangements afforded them opportunities for intercourse. Next came the master of the ship, one Gargiulo, who spoke of the Queen stooping over the bed of Pergami on board the ship. He admitted that the British Ambassador at Naples arranged that he should be paid 1,000 dollars a month to give evidence. Pietro Cuchi, a servant at a Trieste inn at which the accused couple stayed together with the Countess Oldi, Pergami's sister (who accompanied them on their travels), told the House how he spied through a keyhole. Frau Kress, a servant at a Carlsruhe hotel, where the Queen had stayed, did mention a specific incident of importance if true. She said she saw Pergami in bed embracing the Queen, who was sitting on the bed. Cross-examination by Brougham and certain peers cast doubts on her story.

It would be tedious to review all the evidence brought against the Queen. Dr. Stephen Lushington (later the ecclesiastical court judge) had little difficulty in disposing in cross-examination of Raggazoni, a mason, who happened to see the Queen and Pergami together at the Villa d'Este, on Lake Como, which she had set up as a residence. Raggazoni had been ordered to make a statement at Milan by the government. Giuseppe Sacchi, who was courier and equerry to the Queen for a year, spoke of an act of gross intimacy between her and Pergami in the travelling carriage. Louisa Dermont, the Swiss *femme de chambre* of the Queen in Europe, described incidents which pointed to an undue intimacy between the Queen and Pergami at the Villa d'Este and elsewhere. The Queen had dismissed her in 1817. The cross-examination of Dermont and certain other witnesses tended to show that the circumstances in which they made their preliminary statements and were induced to come to these shores were calculated to raise doubts about their credibility.

The Solicitor-General in his review of the evidence against the Queen (referred to as the Princess throughout the trial so far as her conduct in Europe was concerned) cited the well known dictum of Lord Stowell in *Lovedon* v. *Loveden*[1] to the effect that in a case of this nature there was no necessity to prove the actual fact of adultery, for that could not be proved in ninety-nine cases out of a hundred. The rule was that where the facts proved directly led to a conclusion of adultery such proof sufficed.

Brougham followed with an eloquent address, with deft appeals to popular sentiment. As regards the Queen's consorting with inferior people during her travels, he urged that before she left England she was deserted by the peers and peeresses whom she had entertained. In Europe she was received by three sovereigns. He pointed out that all the supposed misconduct alleged against the Queen and Pergami was exposed to the general gaze of many servants and others. Every witness had gone through the drilling and discipline of a Milan tribunal. At that storehouse of false swearing every witness was regularly initiated. Many of them were maintained abroad and in England, at an enormous rate. The witness Sacchi lived a long time in England, enjoying the luxury of a field marshal.

Brougham's analysis of that part of the evidence relating to alleged occasions of endearment and indecorous behaviour of

[1] (1810) 2 Hagg. Con. 1. 4.

the Queen in Pergami's presence gave full rein to his faculty of sarcasm. He said that the most distinguished of their lordships might on the morrow be placed in the situation of one so charged, and must be convicted if a perjured scoundrel was to be believed upon such a principle of selection and separation of evidence. His peroration included the notable passage:

The evidence is inadequate to prove any proposition; impotent to deprive the lowest subject of any civil right; ridiculous to establish the least offence; scandalous to support a charge of the highest nature; monstrous to ruin the honour of the Queen of England.

Much else in this powerful address may be presumed to have swayed the minds of the peers. Witnesses for the Queen included several gentlemen who had seen her at the Villa d'Este and elsewhere on her travels, such as Lord Guilford, son of Lord North; Lord Glenbervie, son-in-law of Lord North; Lady Charlotte Lindsay who conceded that, as Princess, Caroline had always treated servants with a measure of familiarity and condescension. One and all denied that they saw any comprising conduct between Caroline and her retainer Pergami.

Sir William Gell, a classical expert, made light of the suggestion that when the Queen figured as 'the Genius of History' at a *bal masqué* at Naples her costume was indecorous; she was fully clothed as if a statue of Minerva. Baron Ompteda, a Hanoverian envoy at the Vatican, was mentioned as a spy on Caroline, whose confidence he tried to win and whose servants he approached. Another witness employed by the Queen denied that Pergami travelled alone with her in the carriage; his sister Countess Oldi sat between them and later the *femme de chambre*, Dermont.

One witness for the defence Lieutenant J. R. Hownam, R.N., joined Caroline's retinue and went with her on her sea trip to Africa. He said that he challenged Baron Ompteda, the alleged spy, on Caroline's suggestion, but the duel never took place. Questioned by Lord Combermere, the famous cavalry leader in the Peninsular War (during the many sittings a large number of

79

questions were put by peers to witnesses), Lieutenant Hownam said he did not remember Caroline dancing as the Columbine in a harlequinade, though she took the part of the automaton. He denied in examination-in-chief that he had seen any familiarities between Caroline and Pergami aboard ship, but in cross-examination he said he believed Pergami did sleep in her tent on deck, because of the need for a man to be near her in case of a rough sea. There were those who deemed this sailorman's evidence to be damning against the Queen.

Mr Denman's final address for the Queen (ten hours as compared with Brougham's five), though very effective in a further illumination of the evidence, included what seemed to be an oblique comparison of the King's conduct with that of the Emperor Nero in his outrageous treatment of his wife, Octavia. For this he gave mortal offence to the King.[1] He said that Pergami had not been called for the defence because it was contrary to practice for those accused of adultery to appear as witnesses. But he rather spoiled the effect of his address by an unfortunate peroration in which he said:

If your lordships have been furnished with powers . . . to arrive at the secrets of this female, it is your duty to imitate the justice, beneficence and wisdom of that benignant Being, who, not in a case like this where innocence is manifest, but when guilt was detected, and vice revealed, said: 'If no accuser can come forward to condemn thee, neither do I condemn thee; go, and sin no more.'

Those inconsistent remarks led to the much publicised epigram:

Most gracious queen, we thee implore
To go away and sin no more;
Or if that effort be too great,
To go away at any rate.

Dr Lushington in the third final address for the Queen rendered a close analysis of the pros and cons. The Attorney-General

[1] Denman, however, survived the royal wrath to draft the Reform Bill, became Lord Chief Justice in 1832 and a peer in 1834.

(Gifford) followed with an able review of the evidence against the Queen, and Copley, the Solicitor-General, in his concluding address, made great play of Denman's allusion to the precedent of Nero and Octavia, with all its bloodthirsty details.

On 2 November the Lord Chancellor summed up against the Queen. Lord Erskine, the ex-Lord Chancellor, opposed the whole procedure as unconstitutional and questioned the credibility of witnesses called against the Queen before collapsing in his place. Many other peers expressed their views, including Lord Grey who asked the House to find the queen 'not guilty'. The second reading was passed by 123 to 95 votes, but when it came to the third reading on 10 November the Bill gained a bare majority of nine votes—108 to 99. Whether this marked change was due to the popular clamour in favour of the Queen, or to her public 'Protest', in which she declared herself wholly innocent, must be left to conjecture. Lord Liverpool, the Prime Minister, announced the withdrawal of the Bill and by reason of the small majority the Lord Chancellor proposed that the Bill be dropped. A motion passed *nem. con.* accordingly. Thus ended the royal Divorce Bill, one of the most melancholy events in English history.

Sir Shane Leslie in his book, on *George IV* (Benn, 1926), recounts that Brougham had up his sleeve a trump card, proof of the Prince's marriage to Roman Catholic Mrs Fitzherbert, a breach of the Succession Act which might have lost him his throne, if brought to light. The King and some of his coterie were aware of this knowledge and probably the 'trump card', though not played, contributed in no small degree to the fate of the Bill. If it had passed through the House of Lords it would have had to run the gauntlet of the House of Commons.

Queen Caroline was present to hear the result, and emerged to see a thunderous crowd, exulting over her success after the prolonged ordeal. She was excluded, however, from the coronation of George IV though she had driven to Westminster Abbey in State. She died in 1821 at the age of fifty-three.

10 Nineteenth Century

The Napoleonic wars, however little they seemed to affect social life in the upper spheres in England, caused much distress to the working classes, who suffered extreme poverty and even destitution. Poor Law expenditure increased enormously. With such a background, and parliamentary representation almost a farce with its rotten boroughs, public discontent became rife, as education improved throughout the land. Women went to work in the fast-growing factories, a phenomenon which turned out to be a turning-point in family conditions. When the battle of Waterloo signalled the end of the Napoleonic wars the population of Great Britain numbered 13 million an increasing proportion being centred in the industrial towns in England. By 1820 over 1,270,000 people lived in London.

Yet the lot of women in the upper and middle classes remained largely unchanged. 'Ladies' could not go out to work save as governesses, and only then to make a poor sort of living. As Trevelyan wrote, it was the hallmark of a 'lady' to be idle, dabbling in art, poetry and music, but cut off from the more active and useful life of the present day. The man still dominated family life. Despite the husband's marriage vow, 'With all my goods I thee endow', in fact as the law then stood he took all his wife's estate. Prostitutes abounded, and married men as well as single had no hesitation in availing themselves of their services. Yet religious and humanitarian movements were increasing. Slavery was on the way out. The Reform Bill in 1832 opened the door to a more enlightened parliamentary system.

The case of Mrs Caroline Norton brought into prominence the subjugation of married women to the will of their husbands. A talented granddaughter of Sheridan, she was born in 1808. She had two sisters, famous beauties, Helen, a poetess, later Lady Dufferin, and 'Georgy', later Duchess of Somerset. Caroline achieved fame as a poetess, in Byronic style, and earned £1,400 in a year thereby. In 1827 she married the Hon. George Norton, brother of the third Lord Grantley. He filled a small legal post, but thanks probably to his wife's influential connections he became a magistrate. Among her friends were Lord Melbourne, then Secretary of State for Home Affairs. Mr Norton was miserly, coarse and violent to his wife.

After an open rupture he brought an action for *crim. con.* against Lord Melbourne accusing him of adultery with Caroline. The trial took place in 1836, resulting in the acquittal of Lord Melbourne. Sordid disputes followed between the Nortons over money and the custody and care of their children, three sons, claimed by the husband. He did not provide his wife with any maintenance, and in an action claimed her literary earnings from her poems and novels. She wrote pamphlets on English laws for women, on a mother's right to the custody of her children, and on women's social conditions. They had a wide circulation and caused a stir. In 1875 Mr Norton died, and two years later she married Sir W. Stirling Maxwell, but died soon afterwards. A grandson of hers was destined to succeed to the Grantley peerage. It is generally believed that George Meredith made her the prototype of his *Diana of the Crossways*.

Agitation by liberal-minded men and women for a reform in the divorce law gathered pace, and the wide publicity given to a judgment by Mr Justice Maule in the bigamy prosecution, R. v. *Hall alias Robbins,* in 1845 lit up the anomalies, inconsistencies and injustice of the existing system. Many versions of this masterpiece of judicial irony were circulated, long and short.[1] This Assize case

---

[1] The most detailed report is reproduced in Professor McGregor's *Divorce in England*, Heinemann, 1957, from *Marriage Past and Present*, by M. I. Cole, Dent, 1938.

concerned an agricultural labourer whose wife had deserted him after, according to his evidence, she had been guilty of drunken habits and dissipation. The gist of the judgment ran:

Prisoner at the bar, you have been convicted of the offence of bigamy that is to say, of marrying a woman while you have a wife still alive, though it is true that she has deserted you and is living in adultery with another man. You entered into a solemn engagement to take her for better, for worse, and though you appear to have got infinitely more of the latter, it was your duty patiently to submit. You say that you took another person to become your wife because you were left with several young children. Had you taken the other female as your concubine the law would never have interfered with you. You say that you preferred to make an honest woman of her.

You have therefore committed a crime against the law of your country, and acted under a very serious misapprehension of the course which you ought to have pursued. You should have gone to the Ecclesiastical Court and there have obtained against your wife a decree called *a mensa et thoro*. You should then have brought an action in the courts of common law, and obtained a verdict with damages against the other man, though he was not unlikely to be a pauper. But so jealous is the law, which you ought to be aware is the perfection of reason, of the sanctity of the marriage tie, you must then, with your verdict in hand, have approached the Legislature and obtained an Act of Parliament, rendering you free to marry the person you have taken upon yourself to marry with no such sanction.

It would have cost you perhaps five or six hundred or even a thousand pounds, whereas you probably have not as many pence. But it is the boast of the law that it is impartial, and makes no difference between the rich and the poor. You have thus rejected the boon which the Legislature offered you. The sentence of the Court upon you therefore is that you be imprisoned for one day, which period has already been exceeded, as you have been in custody for three days. As a result you will be immediately discharged.

84

When in 1854 Lord Cranworth, Lord Chancellor, introduced a Divorce and Matrimonial Causes Bill, which was later abandoned, he made great play of this judgment.

In 1844 a Select Committee of the House of Lords examined a Bill by Lord Brougham to amend the jurisdiction of the Privy Council on appeals from the ecclesiastical courts. Evidence was given by Dr Stephen Lushington, the eminent judge of the London Consistory Court and of the Admiralty Court, and much of it dealt with the law and procedure in matrimonial causes, and Bills for divorce in Parliament. It was in effect a curtain-raiser for the Commission appointed by Queen Victoria in 1850 under the chairmanship of Lord Campbell (later Lord Chancellor) to inquire into the state of the law of divorce in England and more particularly into the mode of obtaining an absolute divorce. The Commission included Dr Lushington, and Vice-Chancellor (as he became) Sir William Page Wood. The Commission issued its report in 1853, all being in favour of adultery being made a ground for divorce, except Lord Redesdale.

The Common law of England [said the Report], which follows in this case the canon law of the church, 'deems so highly, and with such mysterious reverence, of the nuptial tie', that the causes of Divorce are purposely limited to a few extreme and specific provocations; and the preservation of that union, so long as it can be secured, is so manifestly essential to the best interests of Society, that before it can be dissolved it must be clearly established by the strictest proof that the offence has been committed: that there is no contrivance by which the parties are endeavouring to escape from the solemn obligations to themselves, and their children; that they cannot discharge their mutual duties by continuing any longer to cohabit with each other; and that the party complaining is free from guilt.

Hence have arisen certain well known rules, which the Ecclesiastical Courts have invariably acted upon; as, first that divorce will only be granted for the extreme provocations adverted to above; secondly, that the law will not suffer it to be obtained on the sole confession of the parties themselves; and, thirdly, that it will be refused, even although an offence has been committed, which would otherwise justify it, if collusion, connivance, condonation or recrimination can be pleaded and proved. . . . We conceive that in substance these rules ought to be maintained.

The Report pointed out that a divorce from bed and board left the parties still married, though the wife might be awarded alimony. It was pointed out that before the Reformation a marriage might be annulled for far more extensive causes than since, including pre-contract with some other person, or because the connection was within the degrees of consanguinity or affinity prohibited by the canon law. It was the policy of the Roman Church to multiply impediments to matrimony, the power of granting dispensations having been a fruitful source of ecclesiastical revenue. If a man had carnally known one sister, though not married to her, it would have been incestuous for him to marry, or to have sexual intercourse with, the other sister or even with her relatives by consanguinity or affinity to the eighth degree. Thus it was not by the axe that Henry VIII extinguished his marriage with Anne Boleyn. He first got a sentence from the ecclesiastical court against her for her alleged pre-contract with the Duke of Northumberland, and for his own intercourse with her sister Mary.

The statute 1 Eliz. c. 1. laid down, said the Report, that the only grounds for nullifying and absolving the marriage by reason of antecedent incapacity, were relationship within the forbidden degrees, a previous marriage (not dissolved), corporal imbecility, or mental incompetence. The effects of a sentence nullifying marriage were that the wife lost her dower, children became illegitimate, and the parties freed to marry again.

After a review of the somewhat confused position with regard to divorce *a vinculo* (see Chapter 4), the Commission referred to the 109th canon (1597) which restrained parties who had been granted judicial separation from marrying another person during the lives of the spouses. How far this restraint operated is far from clear. The Commission traced the beginning and development of parliamentary Acts of Divorce, and continued:

The dangerous extremes are absolute and universal indissolubility on the one hand, which has found to be productive of a general connivance at infidelity . . . and on the other a considerable facility of divorce in cases very difficult to be defined—a practice . . . which would be at variance with the institution of marriage, intended chiefly to protect children from the inconstancy of parents, and next to guard wives from the inconstancy of husbands, who, if divorce were procurable for any but clearly defined and most satisfactorily proved facts, would be enabled, as soon as they were tired of their wives, to make the situation of the helpless female so uneasy, that they must consent to divorce.

The Report went on:

It has sometimes been argued that cruelty should have a more extended signification: that other causes of divorce, or, at least, separation from bed and board should be allowed, such as mutual dislike, incompatibility of temper, neglect, severity and repeated provocation . . . The arguments against them are put so forcibly by Lord Stowell, and Hume and Paley, that they are absolutely unanswerable. Lord Stowell says[1]: 'Though in particular cases the repugnance of the obligations of matrimonial cohabitation may operate with great severity on individuals; yet it must be carefully remembered that the general happiness of the married life is secured by its indissolubility.

When people understand that they *must* live together except for a very few reasons known to the law they learn to soften by mutual accommodation that yoke which they know they cannot shake off; they become good husbands and good wives, from the necessity of remaining husbands and wives, for necessity is a powerful master in teaching the duties which it imposes. If it were once understood that upon mutual disgust married persons might be legally separated many couples . . . might at this moment have been living in a state of mutual unkindness, of estrangement from their common offspring, and in a state of the most licentious and unreserved immorality. In this case, as in many others, the

---

[1] *Evans* v. *Evans* (1790), Hagg. Con. 35.

happiness of some individuals must be sacrificed to the greater and more general good . . .

'If it be complained that by the inactivity of the courts much injustice may be suffered, and much misery produced, the answer is that courts of justice do not pretend to furnish cures for all the miseries of human life . . . They cannot make people virtuous; and, as the happiness of the world depends upon its virtue, there may be much unhappiness in it which human laws cannot undertake to remove.'

This great judge was, of course, dealing with only the limited process of divorce *a mensa et thoro*, i.e. judicial separation.

The Commission pointed out that Hume in his essay on 'Polygamy and Divorce', and Paley in his *Moral Philosophy*, laid stress on the same principles, and Hume wrote: 'How many frivolous quarrels and disgusts are there which people of common prudence endeavour to forget, when they be under a necessity of passing their lives together, but which would soon be inflamed into the most deadly hatred, were they pursued to the utmost, under the prospect of an easy separation.'

The Report cited the view of Edmund Burke that the Christian religion by rendering marriage indissoluble had done more towards the peace, happiness, settlement and civilisation of the world than any other part in the whole scheme of divine wisdom. It was submitted that though adultery, desertion and cruelty might justify a separation from bed and board, it did not follow that they would authorise a dissolution of the marriage bond, so as to leave either party to marry again. The door of reconciliation should not be closed. The Commission dealt in detail with the pros and cons of this subject of such grave national importance, before making its final recommendations as follows:

1. Grounds for divorce *a mensa et thoro* conjugal infidelity, gross cruelty; and wilful desertion:

2. Divorce *a vinculo* for adultery only by a wife, who might also apply for divorce *a vinculo* in cases of aggravated enormity such as incest or bigamy:

3. Recrimination, connivance or condonation, if proved, to bar a suit:

4. Existing mode of divorce *a vinculo*, i.e. private Act of Parliament, to be abolished:

5. New civil tribunal to try all questions of Divorce, instead of the ecclesiastical courts, including maintenance of wives and children:

6. Oral evidence in court.

In his minority opinion Lord Redesdale adhered to the doctrine of indissolubility. Following the report Lord Cranworth introduced his Bill in the House of Lords. In his second reading speech in June 1854 he delivered a short historical retrospect on the indissolubility of marriage in the canon law and the numerous expedients sanctioned in Rome for annulling marriages. He argued against divorce by Act of Parliament as an example of the ancient *privilegium,* a special law for each case. He spoke with approval of the passage, of Lord Stowell, quoted heretofore, in *Evans* v. *Evans,* and indicated that the Bill reproduced the recommendations of the Commission. Apart from the question what civil tribunal should take the place of the ecclesiastical courts, the Bill had the general support of Lords Campbell and Brougham, and the reiterated opposition of Lord Redesdale. Eventually the Bill was abandoned, for the purpose of further study, and the preparation of a more elaborate measure.

11 Matrimonial Causes Act 1857

Lord Cranworth introduced the Divorce and Matrimonial Causes Bill in the House of Lords in 1857. The measure proposed that adultery by the wife should be a ground for absolute divorce and adultery by a husband, coupled with cruelty or desertion for two years or more, should entitle the wife to an absolute divorce, and she could claim the same relief on the grounds of his incestuous adultery, his bigamy, and rape, sodomy, or bestiality on his part. Safeguards against deception of the Court in relation to connivance, collusion, condonation and a petitioner's own misconduct were introduced. For the jurisdiction of the ecclesiastical courts the Bill substituted a civil tribunal, but it renewed the old practice and procedure of the ecclesiastical courts for judicial separation, hitherto styled divorce *a mensa et thoro*, and for nullity of marriage.

On the second reading on 19 May 1857 the Lord Chancellor said that nothing would induce him to submit a Bill which would have the slightest tendency to shake the confidence of the country in the permanence of the marriage tie. The fact of that tie being absolutely binding throughout life, except in very extreme cases, was the foundation of the best interest of society. He commented on 'the most extraordinary and ridiculous devices' of the Roman Church to dissolve marriages by way of sentences of nullity and alluded to a statement of Lord Coke that he had known of such a nullity because the husband had stood godfather to a second cousin of his wife. The private Acts of Divorce were too costly except for the richest. He voiced what he called the general feeling at the time that the effect of adultery by a husband was very different from adultery by a wife, but the Bill did not include the ecclesiastical prohibition against a divorced person marrying his or her paramour, although the Bishop of Salisbury invoked the authority of St Augustine to the contrary. He and most of the bishops who took part in the debate opposed the Bill on religious grounds, notably the Bishop of Oxford. Bishop Wilberforce stressed the dangers of collusion, and added that every lawyer would say that if this Bill were passed in the end such causes must go down to the County Courts (a prophecy realised in 1967). If once they entered upon that course it was impossible to say where they would stop. 'The history of every nation', he said, 'showed that increased facility produced increased occasion for divorces, while at the same time morals were lowered, purity sullied, and the honour of married life invaded.'

With reference to revolutionary France in the eighteenth century, he quoted Edmund Burke on the anti-Christian synod then holding its orgies as beginning by breaking down all those restraints that made marriage mysteriously sacred, by granting facilities for divorce which destroyed the only securities for the purity of married life. France, however, taught by the dreadful experience of the past, had long recoiled from the fatal step she had taken. He instanced the example of Prussia, where in the ten years 1820–30 there had been 3,000 divorces in a population of 12 million, that is twenty-seven divorces to each 100,000 people.

Archbishop Sumner (Canterbury), Dr Tait, Bishop of London, and the Bishop of Lincoln came to the aid of the Bill. Lord Lyndhurst, in doing likewise, inveighed in a closely reasoned speech against the inequality of the grounds of divorce as between husband and wife. He said:

No extent of adultery on the part of the husband could, according to this Bill, entitle the wife to a divorce; and hence the trite observation that men made the laws and women were the victims . . .

Suppose that a man lived in open, flagrant, notorious adultery, without disguise or limitation in point of time—perhaps bringing his paramour home to his own wife, insulting her in this way and treating her with great harshness and cruelty, in such case was a wife to be left without a remedy? The husband . . . might violate every human law and yet there would be no divorce (for the wife).

As regards any fear that to allow a wife to divorce her husband on the sole ground of adultery would loosen the marriage bond Lord Lyndhurst said:

Every man who has studied the female character must know that nothing but a long deliberate hopeless suffering—nothing but intolerable agony would overcome her patient endurance— would induce her to come to the court for a divorce. She loses her home, perhaps her position in society, and in all probability the guardianship and care of her children she forfeits by divorce.

Lord Lyndhurst had referred to the fact that in Scotland divorce was granted by the civil courts, and the Duke of Argyll pointed out, on the question of costs, that during four years the Edinburgh Court of Session had pronounced ninety-five judgments of divorce, all for humble folk except one lady of rank.

The second reading of the Bill was passed by 47 votes to 18, a majority of 29, and the third reading by 46 to 25 votes, a majority of 21. It would be wearisome for the reader to report all the arguments *pro* and *con* reproduced in very many columns of Hansard reporting the proceedings in both Houses of Parliament. Suffice it to say that Sir Richard Bethell (later Lord Chancellor Westbury) moved the second reading in the House of Commons on 30 June 1857.

Mr Gladstone, who at that time was out of office, gave vent to one of his prolonged orations in opposition to the Bill. He cited Lord Stowell on the religious character of marriage, and the solemn vows in church. He referred with regret to the practice of the House of Lords in private Acts of Divorce in ignoring its own

Standing Order that it was not lawful for a guilty party to inter-marry with the adulteress. In a disquisition on theological aspects of the subject he claimed that the Council of Trent has declared marriage indissoluble independently of its sacramental character.

He referred to the evils of prostitution in England as nowhere worse in the world, and added:

With regard to another most dangerous evil, namely ante-nuptial incontinence, its prevalence is so general in country as well as in towns, that we must feel humbled to the dust when we consider with how little strictness Christian obligations are in that respect observed. How singular it is that a deplorable laxity with respect to chastity before marriage should be coupled with extraordinary strictness (in the lower classes of society) in the observance of marriage vows ... it is attributable to the indissolubility of marriage according to the English law.

Mr Gladstone, however, always a devout churchman, did persuade the Government to insert a clause whereby no clergyman should be compelled to celebrate marriage by a divorced person to another.

Among those who supported the Bill was Sir George Grey, the Home Secretary, a sound and persuasive speaker, and Mr Spencer Walpole, one of the Commissioners appointed in 1853. The Bill passed its second reading by 208 votes to 97, majority 111, in the House of Commons, and numerous columns of *Hansard* testify to the detailed debates in Committee. However, when the Bill attained its third reading, the main principles survived, much of the arguments having concerned the nature of the civil tribunal to be set up. Numerous amendments to the Bill caused considerable delay in the final passage of the Bill owing to their being brought backward and forward in both Houses. The Royal Assent was given on 28 August 1857, and the Act came into force on 1 January 1858.

Again it is relevant in considering this monumental change in the law of divorce to look at the state of society in England since the young Queen had come to the throne in 1837. Brought up in a court and an aristocracy in which loose living was all too common, Her Majesty soon began to set a tone for the better, and after her marriage to Prince Albert they both became examples to the nation as a whole of improved morals and an impeccable family life. A standard of conduct for society emanated from the highest quarters, which, despite the oft-repeated charges of hypocrisy against the Victorian era, did not fail to preserve the outward decencies.

In a preface to the first three volumes of Queen Victoria's selected letters, published in 1907, Viscount Esher wrote:

The development of the Queen's character is clearly indicated in the papers. We see one of highly vigorous and active temperament, of strong affections, and with a deep sense of responsibility . . . We see her character expand and deepen, schooled by mighty experience into patience and sagacity and wisdom.

The Queen had an all-seeing eye and required her Ministers to keep her well-informed of affairs concerning the state. There is a letter from Lord Granville reporting the debate in the House of Lords on the second reading of the Divorce Bill in 1857. It fell to the lot of Lord Palmerston as Secretary of State to make the usual official report of the second reading debate in the House of Commons. *Inter alia* he wrote that Mr Gladstone (at that time a leading figure in the Tory party) opposed the Bill 'in a speech of two-and-a-half hours, fluent, eloquent, full of theological learning and scriptural research, but fallacious in argument, and with parts inconsistent to each other'.

What her Majesty's views were at the time is not disclosed in her published letters, but after the Act had been in force for over a year, she was constrained to protest at the voluminous reports of divorce suits in the Press. She wrote on 26 December 1859 to the Lord Chancellor, Lord Campbell, of the desirability of preventing publicity of proceedings in the Divorce Court. She wrote:

These cases, which must necessarily increase when the new law becomes more and more known, fill almost daily a large portion of the newspapers, and are of so scandalous a character that it makes it almost impossible for a paper to be trusted in the hands of a young lady or boy. None of the worst French novels from which careful parents would try to protect their children can be as bad as what is daily brought and laid upon the breakfast table of every educated family in England, and in effect must be most pernicious to the public morals of the country.[1]

The Lord Chancellor instituted an inquiry as a result of which a Bill was introduced in Parliament for the limitations of newspaper reports, but the Bill was lost, and Lord Campbell had to inform the Queen that he was helpless.

So the matter rested until in the 1920s a case arousing great interest was reported in some newspapers with such a wealth of frank detail concerning the conjugal relations of a married couple that gave vent to a public outcry. Although in these days sexual details are often unblushingly discussed in all classes of society, the reports of this case in certain newspapers with wide circulations tended to appeal to the prurient and excite adolescents. A movement followed in Parliament as a result of which the Judicial Proceedings (Regulation of Reports) Act 1926 became law. This Act forbade the publication in relation to any judicial proceedings of any indecent matter or indecent medical, surgical or physiological details which would be calculated to injure public morals. Incidentally, as was pointed out at the time, the existing common law already prohibited this, except in technical publications, and on the whole the Press had imposed reasonable limitations on itself. But the Act went on to forbid:

In relation to any judicial proceedings for dissolution of marriage, for nullity of marriage, or for judicial separation or for restitution of conjugal rights, any particulars other than: (i) the names, addresses and occupations of the parties and witnesses; (ii) a concise statement of the charges, defences, and countercharges in support of which evidence has been given; (iii) submissions on any point of law arising in the course of proceedings, and the

[1] *Letters of Queen Victoria* (1970), Vol. III, 482.

decision of the court thereon; (iv) the summing-up of the judge and the finding of the jury (if any) and the judgment of the court and observations made by the judge in giving judgment.

As a consequence the volume of newspaper reports of matrimonial causes perceptibly lessened, and polite euphemisms toning down some robust judicial utterances became general.

So in the course of three centuries or so Parliament enacted more or less the divorce law proposed by the Reformatio Legum Ecclesiasticarium in Tudor times, the main grounds being the wife's adultery on the husband's petition and the husband's adultery, coupled with either cruelty, or desertion for upwards of two years, on the wife's petition. The remedy of judicial separation was open to either spouse on the alternative grounds of adultery, cruelty or desertion for two years or more.

As a safeguard connivance at adultery and collusion calculated to defeat the ends of justice or to deceive the Court, judges were granted powers to investigate any cases where a suspicion of such dealings arose. By the Matrimonial Causes Act 1860 the Queen's Proctor in his capacity as Procurator-General was invested with the power of examining cases brought to his notice and, if advised by the Attorney-General, of intervening, that is, of calling on a petitioner to show cause why a decree *nisi* of divorce should not be rescinded. In addition any individual could intervene in the same way on cause shown. Although under the 1857 Act a decree of divorce had been final, the Act of 1860 provided an interval of three months before the decree could be made absolute, thus giving the Queen's Proctor time for any necessary inquiries. A further Matrimonial Causes Act in 1866 extended the period of delay to six months, but in 1946 this was reduced to six weeks. In special circumstances, such as saving a coming child conceived in adultery being rendered illegitimate the judge could expedite the decree absolute, and it is not unusual for a judge to order the decree *nisi* to be made absolute within a week or less in suitable cases.

At times the Queen's (or the King's) Proctor was called upon to intervene on points of law arising out of individual cases, such as: the jurisdiction of the Indian courts in divorce when India was still a part of the British Empire; the period of gestation before birth; the jurisdiction of the English court when a man deserts his wife and acquires a foreign domicile, a question later settled by the Matrimonial Causes Act 1937 in favour of a deserted wife; the quality of connivance at adultery; the revival of con-doned adultery by desertion which led to a later Act abolishing the doctrine of revival applied to condonation of adultery; whether refusal of marital intercourse constitutes desertion; and whether the use of contraceptives bars a plea in a nullity suit of wilful refusal to consummate the marriage. Interventions by the Queen's Proctor are comparatively few. Over 44,000 decrees *nisi* of divorce were pronounced in 1967. The Proctor, as he is now styled, intervened in sixty-two cases, twenty-nine of which were rescinded as a result.

The question of maintenance of wives and children after divorce began to trouble the public conscience much more than before, and when all the previous Matrimonial Causes Acts were consolidated in a separate part of the Judicature (Consolidation) Act 1925, the principles for the award of maintenance were clearly enunciated. This Act reproduced what had been considered an important safeguard for the court—that it was not bound to grant a decree if the petitioner had committed adultery during the marriage or had delayed unreasonably in presenting the petition, or had treated the other spouse with cruelty, or had deserted him or her, or had conduced to the other's adultery. This power was perpetuated in later Matrimonial Causes Acts, including the consolidating act of 1965.

Turning for a moment to the social background of England in the late 1850s, we see that marked changes were beginning. Various causes combined to improve the condition and education of the working classes, though it was not until Forster's Act, 1870, conferred the boon of primary education for all, so that at any rate the three R's could be instilled into the brains of countless children. The emancipation of women from male subjection was not yet, but the sequel to the Crimean War and the efforts of Florence Nightingale bore fruit in a new professional outlet for women, that of nursing. The upper and middle classes, in a social atmosphere permeated not only with the pervading influence of the Queen but also with the surge of religious and evangelical principles, gave family life a tone, which, despite many latterday accusations of moral hypocrisy and prudery, supported the standard set up by the Queen. Bagehot paid eloquent tribute to this feature in his work on the English Constitution in 1865.

In regard to divorce guilty parties in general earned a stigma, which often cut them off from relations and friends, and for the upper classes from court circles. Indeed to be involved as guilty parties in a divorce meant political ruin for members of Parliament, as witness the fates of Sir Charles Dilke, a potential Prime Minister, following his affair with Mrs Crawford, and of Charles Stewart Parnell, the Irish leader, because of Mrs O'Shea, in the last generation of the Victorian era. Dilke entered the House of Commons years later but never attained ministerial office again, although regarded as one of our most distinguished statesmen.

What has often been depicted on stage, film and television of the tyrannical treatment of his family by Edward Moulton Barrett, who refused to receive his daughters Elizabeth and Henrietta after they married against his will, and died unreconciled to them, is now seen as the typical mastery of a Victorian over his family. He had twelve children and was reputed to have been a kindly father to them when young, though requiring absolute obedience. Doubtless this tutelage, especially of his daughters, in part affected the manifold writings of Elizabeth Barrett Browning in favour of the emancipation of women, although before her marriage in 1846 she had shown tender affection for her father.

A propos of Harriet Beecher Stowe's detestation of slavery in *Uncle Tom's Cabin* (1851), Elizabeth Browning, already a prominent name in literature, wrote to a friend: 'Is it possible that you think that a woman has no business with a question like slavery? Then she had better subside into slavery and concubinage herself, and as in the times of old shut herself up with the Penelopes in the "women's apartment", and take no rank among thinkers and speakers.' She was indignant over the limited scope of well-to-do girls at that time. In her famous blank-verse poem, *Aurora Leigh*, which caused a stir in the late 1850s, and was regarded as an inspiration for women longing to escape from parental discipline, she wrote:

The honest earnest man must stand and work,
the woman also—otherwise she drops
at once below the dignity of man,
accepting serfdom. Free men
freely work.

Elizabeth Browning was echoing the opinions of other celebrated writers and essayists, men and women, in the mid-Victorian period.

Let us turn to the immediate result of the Divorce Act of 1857. The average annual number of decrees *nisi* granted during the first three years of its operation was 141, gradually increasing until 1882–86 when it was 349, and for 1900–10 it was about 620. Divorce remained, however, the luxury of the rich, there being few 'paupers'' cases.

Meanwhile public attention was beginning to fasten on the woes of those members of the working classes to whom divorce was a remedy beyond their means, to the many deserted wives and children who were left unsupported by husbands and fathers. Miss Frances Power Cobbe's powerful appeals in favour of separation orders by magistrates for cruelly treated and deserted wives had their effect. The Matrimonial Causes Act 1878 provided orders for maintenance and custody in such cases, and the Matrimonial Causes Act 1884 for maintenance orders on decrees for restitution of conjugal rights disobeyed by their husbands. Incidentally the old right of sending a spouse to prison for disobeying an order for restitution or of compelling one spouse to return to the other was abolished long ago. The Maintenace of Wives (Desertion) Act 1886 followed, further extending orders for neglect to maintain and desertion. All these provisions were consolidated in the summary Jurisdiction (Married Women) Act 1895, and the Licensing Act 1902, made habitual drunkards liable to such orders.

In progressive stages the right of a married woman to their own property had been established, and the Married Women's Property Act 1882 accorded wives extra facilities for realising such rights in matrimonial disputes concerning their property. This of course was in addition to the law relating to maintenance of wives and children after divorce, judicial separation, and restitution of conjugal rights conferred by the Matrimonial Causes Acts.

A judgment in 1906 by Sir Gorell Barnes, President of the Probate, Divorce and Admiralty Division, which ran to three-and-a-half columns in *The Times*, was the forerunner of a Royal Commission set up in 1909. The case itself raised a problem of jurisdiction, which as the law stood, involved the dismissal of the wife's petition for divorce. As already stated, a wife could obtain a divorce on the ground of adultery coupled with cruelty or with desertion for upwards of two years. She was granted by magistrates a separation order on the ground of her husband's neglect to maintain her in 1896. Later she found out that he had committed adultery, and sued for divorce on the dual grounds of adultery and desertion. Although the then Attorney-General, appearing for the King's Proctor, urged that the separation order was permissive as regards the wife and not compulsory on her, the President held that the order terminated the desertion and dismissed the petition.

Sir Gorell Barnes's weighty dicta at the end of his judgment read as follows:

That the present state of the English law of divorce is not satisfactory cannot be doubted. The law is full of inconsistencies, anomalies, and inequalities almost amounting to absurdities; and it does not produce desirable results in many important aspects. Whether any and what remedy should be applied raises extremely difficult questions, the importance of which can hardly be overestimated, for they touch the basis on which society rests, the principle of marriage being the fundamental basis upon which this and other civilised nations have built up their social systems, It would be most detrimental to the best interests of family life, society and the state, to permit divorce being lightly and easily obtained, or to allow any law wide enough to militate by its laxity against the principle of marriage.

This judgment brings prominently forward the question whether . . . any reform would be effective and adequate which did not abolish permanent separation distinguished from divorce, place the sexes on an equality as regards offence and relief, and prevent a decree from being obtained for such grave causes of offence as render future cohabitation impracticable and frustrate the object of marriage; and whether such reform would not largely tend to greater propriety and enhance the respect for the sanctity of the marriage tie which is so essential in the best interests of society and the state . . . There appear to be good reasons for reform, and probably it should be found to be in the directions I have indicated.[1]

[1] *Dodd* v. *Dodd, The Times,* 28 April 1906.

12 Royal Commission 1909

In 1901 the Victorian era ended with the death of the Queen after a reign of sixty-four years. Great changes had taken place in the face of England in the previous generation. Public education had improved so much that illiteracy among the working classes was exceptional. In upper strata of society girls were no longer kept in the straitjacket of convention limiting their chances of employment. Sophia Jex-Blake, Miss Frances Buss with her school in Camden Town, and other cultured women led the way. Gradually and with difficulty women entered the medical profession and the civil service. They had already begun to play serious lawn tennis, despite the handicap of long skirts, and girls indulged in lacrosse, hockey and other athletic games, without it being considered indecorous.

In general at the turn of the century high society still retained its aristocratic traditions. The great houses with their butlers and servants continued to hold their grand receptions. The middle-classes still had their staff of servants. But there was much poverty among the lower classes.

Subjects that had long been taboo in polite circles, such as sex and birth control in marriage, were discussed in print and in drawing rooms. Already in 1897 Mrs Annie Besant and Charles Bradlaugh had been arraigned for their frank views on birth control, and Havelock Ellis and others gave a fresh impetus to the grave consideration of the sexual functions. The influence of Dr Marie Stopes in regard to contraception was still to come.

When the Royal Commission on Divorce was appointed in 1909 the question of sex equality in regard to offence and relief was very much to the fore. As already stated Sir Gorell Barnes, one of the most eminent Presidents in the Divorce Court of all time, became Chairman. The Commission included the Archbishop of York, Cosmo Gordon Lang (later Archbishop of Canterbury); J. A. Spender, the distinguished editor of the *Westminster Gazette*; Sir William Anson, a famous academic lawyer; Sir Lewis Dibdin, Judge of the ecclesiastical Arches Court, and Sir Rufus Isaacs, K.C., on becoming Solicitor-General, whose place was later taken by Sir Frederick Treves, the Royal surgeon.

The terms of reference called for an inquiry into the state of the law and the administration thereof in divorce and matrimonial causes, and applications for separation orders, especially with regard to the position of the poorer classes in relation thereto, and the subject of the publication of reports of such causes and applications, and to report whether any and what amendments should be made in such law and administration.

This Commission heard many witnesses, including Lord Mersey and Mr Justice Bargrave Deane, respectively a President and Judge of the Divorce Court, Sir Edward Carson, K.C., Sir Edward Clarke, K.C. and several regular Divorce Court counsel, and Sir Frederick Pollock, the famous jurist. After many sittings and much evidence from lawyers, clergy and theologians, sociologists, and doctors, the Commission reported in November 1912 in a comprehensive survey of the whole subject. The majority report recommended that, in addition to adultery the grounds of divorce should be extended to desertion for upwards of three years; cruelty; incurable insanity after five years in confinement; habitual drunkenness found incurable after three years from the first order of separation; and imprisonment under a commuted death sentence.

In regard to nullity of marriage the majority proposed, in addition to existing grounds, where a spouse is of unsound mind at the time of the marriage, or is in a state of incipient mental unsoundness, which becomes definite within six months after marriage, of which the other spouse was then ignorant, provided that the suit be instituted within one year of marriage, and there has been no marital intercourse after discovery of the defect; where a spouse at the time of the marriage is suffering from a venereal disease in a communicable form, and the fact is not disclosed to the other spouse who remains ignorant of the fact, with a similar proviso; and where a woman is found to be pregnant at the time of her marriage, her condition being due to intercourse with some man not her husband, and her condition has not been disclosed to him, with a similar proviso.

The minority report, signed by the then Archbishop of York, Sir William Anson and Sir Lewis Dibdin, rejected the extension of grounds of divorce, but were willing to approve the proposed additional grounds for nullity.

Other important proposals in the majority report were that husbands and wives should be on an equal footing as regards the grounds of divorce; that a married person should be entitled to obtain an order presuming the death of a vanished spouse, coupled with a decree of divorce; that a decree absolute of divorce should be unimpeachable after five years from its pronouncement; and that the Court in its discretion should be empowered when a decree of judicial separation is claimed on grounds found by the Court which would justify a divorce, to make a decree of divorce on the application of the respondent.

By this time there had been a gradual increase in the number of divorces. In 1867 petitions numbered 233 and decrees *nisi* 119. The annual average of decrees *nisi* between 1868 and 1875 was about 200. Between 1876 and 1899 the annual number varied from 267 to 525, showing a progressive increase from the year 1892. As already stated the annual average for 1900–10 was about 620.

Statistics and percentages per population have to be carefully scrutinised and are often misleading as any 1,000 of population includes children and single persons. Petitions in any one year outnumber decrees *nisi* and not all of the latter are made absolute. Suffice it to say that, when the Royal Commission reported, the ratio of divorces to marriages in any one year was negligible, and scarcely threatened the social structure.

Returning to the Royal Commission's Majority Report in 1912 we find that there were other recommendations, some of which, as narrated hereafter, became law after the passage of years, for example, that the grounds for judicial separation should be the same as for divorce; and the same defences should be available; that proceedings *in forma pauperis* should be more readily available; and that restrictions be imposed on the publication of newspaper reports of divorce suits (see Chapter 11).

The minority report uttered a note of warning, which has often been repeated by sage counsellors since when more and more increases in divorce facilities have been mooted. They wrote:

Experience shows that on the whole increase of facilities and grounds of divorce lead to domestic instability. There is abundant evidence that the classes mainly affected by the Divorce Court are becoming less careful of the restraint and the obligations of family life. This certainly seems to be the effect of divorce legislation in the United States.

They referred to the remarkable words of President (Theodore) Roosevelt when he said: 'There is a widespread conviction that the divorce laws are dangerously lax and indifferently administered in some of the States, resulting in a diminishing regard for the sanctity of the marriage relation.' They added:

There can be no question that hitherto the strength of English social life has been the family—the home. The evidence is re-assuring that among the great bulk of the people, especially among the middle-class and artisans, the obligations of marriage are respected, and home life is pure and consistent. The reason for this state of things is the general social conviction that marriage binds those who enter into it for better or for worse. It is a life-long obligation with all the sacrifice which such an obligation involves. Our contention therefore is that the State, in its own interest, should maintain and not relax the standard of its present marriage law ... The causes of marriage failure are, speaking generally, the lack of the sense of responsibility in entering the married state, and the lack of self-control, self-sacrifice, and the sense of duty in continuing it. To attempt to deal with these matters by multiplying grounds of divorce is surely to attack the problem at the wrong end.

The minority deprecated a proposal that county court judges should have jurisdiction in certain localities.

Governments in this country have been notoriously loath to tackle the problem of divorce, preferring to give a trial run to a private member's Bill, and if it seems to catch the popular fancy to take it up.

However, after 1912 the Government were mainly concerned with the problems of a belligerent Germany and Home Rule for Ireland. In August 1914 the lights went out and the first world war began. No steps having been taken by Parliament to implement any of the Royal Commission's Report the grounds of divorce remained the same as in the 1857 Act, that is, a husband could divorce his wife on the ground of adultery, and a wife could divorce her husband on the grounds of adultery coupled with cruelty or desertion for two years or more, or of certain perverse practices.

This inequality of remedy between the sexes was much criticised, and is illustrated in Galsworthy's *Forsyte Saga*. It will be remembered that the wife of Soames Forsyte left her husband after she had fallen in love with a young architect. Soames took no action until twelve years later; desperate to get an heir of his blood to his wealth, he implored his wife to afford him grounds for divorce. Her desertion was undoubted but that *per se* was no ground for divorce. So she threw in her lot with a cousin of Soames, young Jolyon Forsyte, and Soames got a divorce on the double ground. It was not until 1923 that a further short Matrimonial Causes Act was passed giving a wife the right to divorce her husband on the ground of adultery alone.

In 1913 the number of divorces granted in England and Wales was 577, but owing to the social disruption arising out of the war of 1914–18 the number increased fourfold. In 1915 there were 1,060 decrees *nisi*, in 1919, 2,630, and in 1937 over 5,000. Taking the annual average of persons who married at about 350,000 the ratio of divorces to marriages was only one to seventy. Yet the Divorce Court with only a President and another judge found it difficult to deal with so many divorce suits, and more judges had to be appointed in this Division of the High Court. Moreover, the rush of divorce at the end of the war was met by bringing in the Lord Chancellor (Lord Birkenhead) and some retired judges to cope with it.

Women had been brought in to aid in the manufacture of munitions, and they had made their mark also in the armed services. It was largely due to their national work during the war that they were so willingly granted the parliamentary vote in 1918, though Mrs Pankhurst and other suffragettes had paved the way with their demonstrative activities before the war began. Thus the mixing of the sexes and the general change in social relations occasioned by the war gave rise to a feverish outlook by large parts of the population. The extravagances of the 'Jazz Age' and the 'Bright Young Things' on the one hand, and grievous unemployment on the other have passed into history. The day of the motorcar, with so many rushing about from place to place, helped to unsteady social life.

Unsuccessful efforts had been made in Parliament to give effect to certain recommendations in the Royal Commission's Report 1912 by Lord Gorell (son of the Chairman), Lord Buckmaster (ex-Lord Chancellor) and Mr Holford Knight, M.P. Finally Mr (later Sir) Alan P. Herbert, brought in his private member's Bill in the house of Commons to change the law of divorce. He was M.P. for Oxford University, elected in 1935. His industry and skill in at first introducing a Bill on such a controversial subject, which no Government dared to touch, may be discovered in his amusing book *The Ayes Have It* (Methuen, 1937). His Bill originally contained certain proposals which were either dropped in Committee of the House of Commons or rejected or amended in the House of Lords. But by the time it reached the Upper House it had the general support of the Government. In July 1937 the Bill, considerably amended, received the Royal Assent.

It introduced a new feature into the Divorce Law, intended to propitiate the Church and the bishops and reconcile them to the other changes, most of them recommended by the Royal Commission in 1912. A restriction was imposed on petitions for divorce being presented during the first three years after marriage, subject to a judge giving leave for such a petition on the grounds of exceptional hardship being suffered by the petitioner during the three years or of exceptional depravity by the respondent within that period. In determining such applications to petition before the end of the triennial period the judge is required to consider the interests of any children of the marriage and the possibility of a reconciliation between the spouses.

The Act placed the sexes on an equal footing with regard to the grounds of divorce, namely adultery, desertion for three years or more, cruelty, and incurable unsoundness of mind.

The time-honoured safeguards against fraud or deception of the Court were perpetuated, by requiring the judge to satisfy himself that there has been no connivance at adultery, no collusion between the parties, or no condonation of adultery or cruelty, or no unreasonable delay in presenting the petition, or no conduct by the petitioner conducing to the matrimonial offence alleged. The grounds for judicial separation became the same as for divorce, with leave to the petitioner to be granted a decree of divorce later if he or she so decided.

Another new feature affected the procedure for nullity of marriage. In addition to the old well-established grounds of nullity a decree therefore might be obtained because of the wilful refusal of a spouse to consummate the marriage, or that at the time of the marriage a spouse was a mental defective or subject to recurrent fits of insanity or epilepsy, or suffering from a communicable venereal disease, or pregnant by some third party. These new grounds were subject to certain restrictions to defeat any abuse of the procedure, and to a condition according legitimacy to children of the unions so annulled.

The recommendation of the Royal Commission in 1912 was given effect as to a decree for presumption of death, coupled with divorce, against a vanished spouse. The fact that for a period of seven years or upwards the vanished spouse had been continually absent from the petitioner, and the latter had no reason to believe that the party was living within that period was to be accepted as evidence that the vanished spouse was dead, unless there were evidence to the contrary.

If a successful petitioner did not apply for a decree *nisi* to be made absolute, the respondent might apply to have it made absolute. Amendments were also made with regard to maintenance of spouses and children, settlements of property and the like.

To meet the case of wives deserted by their husbands who thereafter go abroad and acquire a foreign domicile jurisdiction was conferred on the Court in divorce suits by wives in such circumstances.

The Act came into force on 1 January 1938, and in that year divorces numbered 6,250. From that year the decrees granted gradually increased, reaching 10,000 in 1943 (midway during the second world war), and 15,600 in 1945. At the end of the war, after the further disruption in social life, an overwhelming rush to the Divorce Court ensued; over 60,000 petitions were launched in 1947 and over 58,380 decrees pronounced in that year.[1] This was the high peak of divorces, and as marriages were more or less constant at an annual average of about 400,000 during the previous ten years we find that the ratio of divorces to marriages was at that time one divorce to seven marriages.

With such a spate of divorces, and though the strength of the Divorce Court judiciary had been necessarily increased, it was still found impossible to cope with the vast number of petitions without calling in outside aid. Accordingly the recommendation in the 1946 Report of a committee under the chairmanship of Mr Justice Denning (now Lord Denning, Master of the Rolls) was adopted whereby selected County Court Judges were summoned to try divorce suits as High Court Commissioners. Moreover selected King's Counsel were appointed *ad hoc* to perform the same duty on the strength of a somewhat ambiguous section in a Judicature Act. A few of the latter continued as temporary High Court Judges for this purpose for many years, on the basis of appointment from term to term. Incidentally the Denning Report

[1] *Statistical Review of England and Wales,* 1949, p. 54.

led to clearing away a lot of procedural dead wood in the Divorce Registry.

Social conditions as the result of the 1939–45 war changed enormously. The working classes improved their status and wages, thanks largely to the increased and increasing powers of the trade unions and the more liberal legislation. The middle-class housewife learned to carry on without servants and the upper classes were not much better off, except for those who had managed to retain or make large fortunes in trade. Although the inevitable admixture of the sexes in war work had taken place throughout, the sequel on the whole was free from the partial demoralisation that followed the first world war.

As life became more settled the number of decrees of divorce fell to 27,353 in 1954. In the meantime the Legal Aid Act 1949 was passed, giving far more financial facilities for divorce than became available under the old Poor Person's Rules. Nevertheless the annual figure of divorces tended to decrease for some years thereafter, the average for 1951–54, however, being about 33,000; for 1957–60 it was reduced to about 23,200. But in 1961 decrees absolute of divorce numbered close on 25,000, after which time the number increased progressively to 37,000 in 1965. Of the petitions presented in 1961 the majority were filed by wives, most of the suits being on the ground of adultery, with desertion or cruelty in about half the cases.

A movement arose for changing the law whereby a divorce might be obtained after a separation of spouses for a specified period of years, as a single ground, and this led to the appointment of a Royal Commission in 1951.

13 Royal Commission 1951-55

A movement having arisen for a further development of the divorce law, Mrs Eirene White, M.P., introduced a private member's Bill in 1951 to allow spouses after seven years' separation to petition for divorce, subject to there being no reasonable prospect of the parties becoming reconciled. The argument was repeated that if in fact the marriage had irretrievably been broken, better that it should be ended, for the sake of the parties and the interest of the State.

But the sting lay in the inference that an innocent wife, who for religious or other reasons refused to divorce a guilty husband, might be compelled to be divorced against her will. The Bill passed its second reading in the House of Commons, but after considerable debate Mrs White withdrew it on the Government's promise to appoint a Royal Commission to examine this proposal and cognate subjects concerning the law of divorce.

Lord Morton of Henryton (then a Lord of Appeal) was appointed Chairman, with several judges experienced in the administration of divorce, Lord Keith (then a Scottish Judge and later Lord of Appeal) Mr Justice Pearce (later a Lord of Appeal), Mr Geoffrey Lawrence, Q.C. (later a High Court Judge), and others, including Sir Frederick J. Burrows, a president of the Law Society, Sir Russell Brain (later Lord Brain) the eminent surgeon, and Mr James Walker, Q.C. (later a Scottish judge).

The terms of reference called on the Commission to inquire into the laws of England and Scotland concerning divorce and other matrimonial causes and into the powers of courts of inferior jurisdiction in matters affecting relations between husband and wife, and to consider whether any changes should be made in the law or its administration, including the law relating to the property rights of husband and wife, both during marriage and after its termination (except by death), having in mind the need to promote and maintain healthy and happy married life and to safeguard the interests and wellbeing of children and to consider whether any alteration should be made in the law prohibiting marriage with certain relations by kindred or affinity.

The Commission heard a very large variety of witnesses with expert evidence of the problems with which it had to deal, including representatives of numerous organisations concerned with the public weal. Its Report (Cmd 9678), published in 1956, ran to 400 pages of a bulky Blue Book, and revealed the great care and scrutiny employed by the Commissioners in dealing with a subject of such great national importance. In a preface to the Report, the Commission emphasised the social factors (already touched upon in previous pages of this book) which had put a strain on married life and, superimposed on the frailties of human nature, had led to a plethora of divorce. They pointed *inter alia* to the scarcity of houses which prevents many young couples from starting married life in houses of their own, and to the casualties so often arising through marriages at too early an age (a grave phenomenon which has had even more serious results since 1956). They stressed the social and economic emancipation of women, no longer content to be the inferior partner, and the tendency to regard the assertion of one's own individuality as a right, reckless of the consequences to others. Moreover, they emphasised a tendency to accept the duties and responsibilities of marriage less seriously, so that there was less disposition to put up with the rubs of daily life.

Some witnesses, the Report said, recommended that the existing grounds of divorce should be abolished and their place taken by a single comprehensive ground which would allow divorce if it could be proved that a marriage had irretrievably broken down. They argued that the matrimonial offences on which divorce was founded under the existing law were not usually the real causes of the breakdown of a marriage but merely its symptoms, and most of these witnesses favoured divorce by mutual consent of the spouses and divorce at the option of either spouse after a period of separation. It was urged that husband and wife should be allowed to terminate their marriage if they so agreed. The advocates of these proposals argued that if a marriage had irretrievably broken down it was in the interests of the spouses and their children, if any, and the community, that divorce should set the parties free to marry again, reducing the risk of illicit unions and illegitimate children.

The Commission, with the sole exception of Lord Walker, agreed that the existing law based on the doctrine of the matrimonial offence should be retained. Nine members of the Commission, Lord Morton, Mr Beloe, Lady Bragg, Lord Brain, Sir F. Burrows, Mr Flecker, Mr Geoffrey Lawrence, Q.C., Mr Mace, a solicitor, and Mr Justice (now Lord) Pearce opposed breakdown of marriage as a ground of divorce as gravely detrimental to the wellbeing of the community.

Nine members of the Commission, Lord Keith, Mrs Allen, Dr Baird, Mrs Bruce, Mr Brown, Mrs Jones-Roberts, Mr Maddocks, Lady Portal, and Mr Young, recommended that after seven years' separation, it should be possible for either spouse to obtain a divorce, if the other did not object. But four of the last-named members went further and proposed that after seven years' separation either spouse could obtain a divorce notwithstanding the other's objection.

The nine members who opposed the principle of breakdown of marriage as the ground of divorce regarded the proposal (Report, para. 69) as containing the seeds of grave damage to marriage as an institution and disastrous to the stability of marriage. The divorce rate would be swollen by the failure of marriages which would otherwise have held together with advantage to both parties as well as to children. People would then come to look on marriage less and less as a lifelong union and more and more as one to be ended if things began to go wrong, and in the end widespread divorce would become an accepted feature of our society, ultimately destroying the concept of lifelong marriage.

They added that if the principle that a marriage should be ended if it has irretrievably broken down is followed to its logical conclusion, it must be accepted that a spouse who had committed no recognised matrimonial offence could be divorced against his will. In their opinion this would be so plainly unjust as to be in itself conclusive against the introduction of any ground of divorce which had this result.

As to the proposals of the four Commissioners the majority concluded that for a spouse who had committed no recognised matrimonial offence to be divorced against his or her will would be plainly unjust; further, that, as marriage is a status, if husband and wife were free to terminate their marriage at pleasure, then marriage would become a mere contract and the interests of the community would receive no recognition and it would be disastrous to the nation. When difficulties arose in married life there would be much less incentive to overcome them. The state would bear the brunt of the responsibility since, in giving its blessing to divorce by consent, it would have encouraged people to abandon their marriages on the flimsiest provocation.

The nine members opposed to the doctrine of breakdown of marriage as a ground of divorce went on:

We believe that it is fundamentally incompatible with the concept of marriage as a union for life of the parties to be free to put an end to it by agreement. A marriage cannot be the concern only of the partners to it. If there are children, their interest must be considered . . . The State has an overriding responsibility to ensure in the interests of the community that the institution of marriage is upheld . . . To give people a right to divorce themselves would be to foster a change in the attitude to marriage which would be disastrous for the nation . . . When difficulties arose in married life (as happens in most marriages) there would be much less incentive to overcome them . . . Divorce would increasingly be sought in circumstances where, if a little effort were made, husband and wife would adjust their differences. Such an attitude would be fatal to stability and security in marriage, which in the end would come to be regarded as a temporary relationship, with

114

divorce as a normal incident of life. The State, in giving its blessing to divorce by consent, would have encouraged people to abandon their marriages on the flimsiest provocation.

Dealing with the condition proposed by the supporters of divorce by consent—that the court must be satisfied that consent was freely given—it was pointed out that it would be impossible to find out if an unwilling spouse had been worn down by pressure into giving a reluctant consent. A weak or self-sacrificing spouse, who genuinely did not want a divorce, would be left virtually unprotected.

Pausing here, it should be explained that there has been generated a public fallacy that nearly all undefended divorce suits are collusive as between the spouses. On the contrary in all such cases, as the law stood in 1968, a matrimonial offence had to be proved whether adultery, cruelty, or desertion for three years or more. Doubtless cases have occurred where people have put their heads together and as a result adultery had been committed, but it is the duty of solicitors and counsel to advise against any such deceitful artifice.

The Commission expressed the view that 'hotel adultery' cases were less frequent than was often supposed. Commenting on an argument which had been advanced that divorce by consent provided a dignified means of release they regarded it as 'most insidious', and said that there could be no subtler temptation to divorce than the belief that there was a wholly blameless way of terminating a marriage.

Dealing with the proposal in Mrs White's Bill that after seven years' separation either spouse should be enabled to divorce the other willy-nilly, the nine opposing members of the Commission, named heretofore, said that it would introduce into the law a principle which would have even more damaging consequences for the institution of marriage than divorce by consent. People would enter marriage knowing that no matter what they did they could always get free. This sense of insecurity and uncertainty would have a most disturbing effect on family life. To vest in a husband or wife the right to divorce a spouse, who *ex hypothesi* had committed no recognised matrimonial offence, would result in grave injustice. It would allow a man who had committed adultery or had been cruel to his wife to leave her and subsequently to divorce her against her will. The wife would have a divorce forced on her. Referring to witnesses who supported this proposal the nine Commissioners pointed to cases where a long and happy marriage was broken by the infatuation of a husband for a younger woman, or a wife was treated with cruelty before her husband deserted her, or a deserted husband was left with a young family to bring up.

Those who wish to examine the arguments of the supporters of divorce by consent must refer to the evidence, not set out but duly considered in the Commission's Report, and to Professor McGregor's *Divorce in England*. Suffice it to say that the National Marriage Guidance Council, where efforts to strengthen the institution of marriage had earned a tribute from the Denning Committee, in its first report to the Royal Commission, stated: 'We are in no doubt that the existence of comparatively easy divorce does tend to lessen respect for marriage and to have an adverse effect on the attitute of those who are marrying or who are experiencing marriage difficulties.'

Apart from the repugnance felt by the nine Commissioners for the doctrine of divorce by consent, and the rejection by the Commission of the proposal that the matrimonial offence basis of divorce should be abolished, substantive recommendations were made in a variety of relevant matters, for example:

1. That wilful refusal by a spouse to consummate the marriage should be an additional ground for divorce and not nullity, as this is an event which follows a valid marriage and does not precede it.

2. Acceptance by a wife of artificial insemination by a donor without her husband's consent should be a ground for divorce or judicial separation. These recommendations have not passed into law.

3. The same in the case of a mental defective who, by reason of dangerous or violent propensities, has been detained in a mental

defectives' institution for at least five years, and whose recovery is highly improbable. This recommendation has led to a change in the law which virtually gives effect to it.

4. Where a married couple have separated before 1 October 1937 (when the Matrimonial Causes Act, 1937, was passed) in circumstances amounting to desertion by one of them, the fact that before that date they agreed to live apart should no longer bar the deserted spouse from petitioning for divorce on the ground of desertion. Statutory effect has been given to this recommendation.

5. In cases of divorces for insanity the requirement of care and treatment should be modified, and the law has been altered accordingly.

6. Reasonable arrangements for maintenance of wives and children, negotiated before divorce, should not operate as a collusion bar, if sanctioned by the court. This also has been passed into law.

7. Condonation of a matrimonial offence should be presumed from any subsequent marital intercourse, but for the purpose of conciliation a trial period during which marital intercourse has occurred should not necessarily amount to condonation. This also has been enacted.

8. Insanity of a spouse charged with cruelty should not be a good defence. Judicial decisions have endorsed this proposal.

9. The Royal Commission also recommended that the State should give every encouragement to conciliation of disputing spouses by grants to existing agencies, and facts learnt by a marriage guidance counsellor should be inadmissible as evidence in any subsequent matrimonial proceedings. Legislative effect has not been given to these proposals.

For the rest the Commission recommended many improvements in divorce for the maintenance of wives and children, and for the welfare of the latter, most of which have been adopted in recent Acts of Parliament, together with changes concerning property rights between husband and wife and matrimonial proceedings in magistrates' courts.

The Commission gave weighty reasons for retaining the exclusive jurisdiction in divorce in the Probate, Divorce and Admiralty Division of the High Court. They endorsed the principle stated as follows in the report of the Royal Commission of 1912:

The gravity of divorce and other matrimonial cases, affecting as they do the family life, the status of the parties, the interests of their children, and the interest of the State in the social and moral wellbeing of its citizens, makes it desirable to provide, if possible, that even for the poorest citizens, those cases should be determined by the superior courts of the country assisted by the attendance of the Bar, which we regard as of high importance in divorce and matrimonial cases, both in the interests of the parties and in the public interest.

The Commissioners in the 1956 Report also agreed with the view of the Denning Committee that the manner in which divorce was effected influenced the attitude of the community towards the status of marriage.

Despite this advice the Matrimonial Causes Act 1967, was passed, not without reasoned opposition, conferring County Court jurisdiction in all undefended matrimonial causes, which constitute the vast majority of such cases. The result is that degrees in divorce and other matrimonial causes are disposed of by the inferior courts, with nearly all their ancillary consequences concerning maintenance and the like.

In 1966 decrees absolute of divorce numbered 38,352 and in 1967 they increased to close on 43,000, a rate of about one divorce to ten marriages, and in 1967 close on 50,000 petitions for divorce were presented.

The proposals put forward for a drastic change in the law of divorce in a private member's Bill in the House of Commons in 1968, substituting the notion of 'irretrievable breakdown of marriage' as the sole ground of divorce instead of a matrimonial offence are considered in Chapters 16 and 17.

14 Jurisdiction and Domicile

Few laymen appreciate what an important rôle domicile plays in their lives, affecting contracts, wills and intestacy, and especially divorce. Every person in English law is supposed to have a domicile, and the law of the country in which he is domiciled usually applies to him. Domicile is the place or sovereign country where he lives with the intention of remaining there. If a person is born in England and Wales or in Scotland and continues to live there without emigrating or going to live abroad he is domiciled in his native country. Likewise if the same thing happens in France or any other country he remains domiciled in that country according to English or Scottish law. Many complications arise under this law, owing to the fact that in most other countries the principle is different. In France, for instance, it is the law of nationality, and not domicile, which applies to the person who under French law becomes a citizen of that country. *Domicil* in French means residence, even if only temporary.

Jurisdiction in divorce in England applies to a husband and his wife domiciled in England, but if the husband settles abroad and thus changes his domicile, neither spouse can sue for divorce in England. There are some statutory exceptions, and others with regard to English people living temporarily abroad, but that is the guiding principle.

Historical development has brought it about that, though a wife nowadays is fully entitled to have separate property, she is treated as coupled with her husband for income tax purposes, similarly she is held to have the same domicile as her husband. This result, which is regarded as normally for her benefit and making for domestic harmony, has been found to cause injustice for a wife in divorce. Formerly if a man deserted his wife and acquired a foreign domicile she could not divorce him in England but had to sue for divorce in the country of his new domicile, generally beyond her means. But the Matrimonial Causes Act 1937 put that right for her so that in such case she can divorce him in England on recognised grounds.

Difficulties with regard to domicile both in divorce and nullity of marriage have led to hundreds of disputed cases on the problem of jurisdiction. In neither class of matrimonial cause has any Act of Parliament definitely laid down rules of jurisdiction for the English and Scottish Courts. It has been left to the judges to decide, and in the main they have founded the principle that divorce can only be granted where the husband is domiciled in England. In nullity suits the jurisdiction of the court differs in some respects.

An attempt was made to clarify the situation by the Royal Commission on Marriage and Divorce in its 1956 Report. A code was drafted, but two Bills for that purpose failed to gain acceptance in Parliament.

In the field of private international law various attempts have been made to reduce the conflict of national laws affecting jurisdiction. One of the most notable was the draft Prague Convention of the International Law Association in 1947, following fifteen years of gestation. In this Convention the grounds for divorce or nullity, which differ widely between country and country, were not touched. All that the Convention proposed was that if a competent court, that is, a tribunal vested with the power of dissolving or annulling a marriage, made a decree in the country (1) in which either the husband or the wife was domiciled when the suit was commended, or (2) in which either spouse had been actually resident for a year next preceding the date of the petition, or (3) of which either party was a national at the time of the petition, any such decree should be recognised in the countries accepting the Convention.

There were minor conditions, but in fact the Convention was not ratified by the British or any other Government. Recently the diplomatic Hague Conference tackled this thorny problem afresh and in 1968 adopted a Convention on the Recognition of Divorces and Legal (i.e. judicial) Separation. Such decrees were to be recognised in the contracting countries if

1. the respondent had his habitual residence in the country where the petition was presented; or

2. The petitioner also had his habitual residence there, and either he had been so resident there for a year next before the date of the petition, or the spouses habitually resided there together; or

3. Both spouses were nationals of that country; or

4. The petitioner was a national thereof, and (a) either had his habitual residence there, or (b) had habitually resided there for a year within two years preceding the date of the petition; or

5. The petitioner for divorce was a national of that country and was there at the date of the petition, and the spouses had last habitually resided together in a country whose law did not provide for divorce.

These were the main conditions, subject to reservations which need not be enumerated in a work of this kind in which technicalities are avoided as far as possible. The Convention was signed by delegates of Austria, Belgium, Canada, Czechoslovakia, Denmark, Eire, Finland, France, Western Germany, Greece, Israel, Italy, Japan, Jugoslavia, Luxemburg, the Netherlands, Norway, Portugal, Spain, Sweden, Switzerland, Turkey, Great Britain, and U.S.A., also the United Arab Republic and Indonesia.

In effect the Convention, if and when ratified by any contracting countries, lays down the mutual recognition of decrees on two bases of jurisdiction proposed by the Prague draft Convention:

more or less permanent residence, and nationality. The Anglo-American conception of domicile as a basis of jurisdiction was excluded from the Convention. This has always been the chief bar against universal mutual recognition of divorces, although recent decisions in the English Courts have tended towards a less strict observance of the domicile principle, for example *Travers* v. *Holley* (1953) Probate 246, in the Court of Appeal, and *Indyka* v. *Indyka* (1969) A.C. 33 in the House of Lords.

In the first cited case the jurisdiction in divorce in New South Wales substantially coincided with the jurisdiction obtaining in England, and therefore the Court of Appeal decided that what entitles an English court to assume jurisdiction must be equally effective in the case of a foreign court, and it would be contrary to principle and inconsistent with comity if the English courts refused to recognise a jurisdiction which *mutatis mutandis* they claimed for themselves; so the Australian decree was held to be valid.

The second case cited, in which the House of Lords upheld the principle in *Travers* v. *Holley*, broke new ground. It was held that where the Czech wife of an Englishman domiciled in England obtained a divorce in Czechoslovakia, the jurisdiction being based on her Czech nationality, and she having lived all her life in that country, continuing to reside there after the divorce, the decree was binding because of her substantial connection with the country of her birth and residence.

The grounds for nullity of marriage in the Roman canon law, which still operate in Eire, Italy, Spain, Portugal, and the other Roman Catholic countries, and those operating in England have been dealt with in Chapter 2, and Chapters 4 and 12 respectively. But the jurisdiction in nullity, as already stated, differs from that of divorce, and owing to conflicting judgments of the superior courts from time to time remains in a state of some confusion. The Law Commission set up by Lord Gardiner, Lord Chancellor, is considering what may seem to be anomalies, with a view to legislation. The number of decrees of nullity in England is negligible in comparison with that of decrees of divorce, but nevertheless people should know where they stand when they petition for a declaration of nullity.

In this connection a new procedure was set up by the Court of Appeal in the case of *Har-Shefi*, Law Reports (1953), p. 161, whereby it was decided that the Divorce Court may make a declaration of status on petition without any obligation to present a petition for divorce or in any other matrimonial cause. This procedure largely does away with the ancient petition for jactitation whereby a person may be forbidden falsely to boast that he or she is married to another person.

The Court's jurisdiction in judicial separation is at present based as far as possible on the procedure of the ecclesiastical courts before 1958, subject to a later impingement upon the principle of domicile. In general it involves the residence of the petitioner in England, but not necessarily of the respondent. But legal complications have arisen about jurisdiction.

In petitions for restitution of conjugal rights, which are still allowed but are soon to be abolished, jurisdiction in England depends as in judicial separation upon residence in England rather than domicile. But it is exercised where the husband's domicile is in England, and where the parties had their matrimonial home in England when they ceased to live together.

Though judicial declarations of legitimacy are not very common the procedure has been available since the Legitimacy Declaration Act 1858, the effect of which has been reaffirmed in subsequent statutes. Anyone who is a British subject, or whose right to be deemed such wholly or in part in his legitimacy or the validity of any marriage, if domiciled in England or Northern Ireland may petition for a decree declaring that he is the legitimate child of his parents, and that the marriage of his father and mother or of his grandfather and grandmother was valid, or that his own marriage was valid.

For the relevant rules for deciding the legitimacy of a person readers must refer to the legal text books such as Dicey's *Conflict of Laws* and *Latey on Divorce*. Unless the petitioner is within the categories set out in section 39 of the Matrimonial Causes Act 1965, the court has no jurisdiction. This is exemplified by the petition of a man for a declaration of legitimation of two uncles, which was dismissed for lack of jurisdiction: *Knowles* v. *Attorney-General* (1951) Probate 54.

The Legitimacy Act 1926 extended both the law and the jurisdiction by providing that anyone who was born before the marriage of his parents became legitimate after the marriage. Thus normally wisdom prompted that he should obtain a judicial declaration to that effect; and a more recent Act provided that he was legitimate despite the fact that his father or mother was married to a third person when the applicant was born. The 1926 Act, however, laid down certain limitations against a legitimated person being entitled to property interest or titles of honour. But otherwise a declaration of legitimacy places the person in whose favour such a decree is made in the same legal position as a person actually born legitimate.

It sometimes happens that a couple may live together for many years, but on their deaths leave it in doubt whether or not they were legally married. In such cases the doctrine of marriage by habit and repute may be followed, and without specific evidence of a ceremony of marriage the court is entitled in a suitable case to presume that a marriage had taken place. This was especially important in regard to irregular marriages in Scotland entered into by agreement of the parties but never officially recorded: this system of irregular marriages in Scotland was abolished in 1940.

Latterly medical blood tests have been approved by the English courts to disprove the supposed progenitor of a child. Both judges and magistrates have become acquainted with the form of deceit, fortunately not frequent, when a pregnant young woman tries to pass off to her husband the responsibility of another man for her condition. Her motive may be either to hide her lapse or to save her lover, perhaps himself married, from exposure.

Most of these blood tests, dependent as they are on the blood groups of the man, woman and child concerned, turn out to be neutral, but in a fair proportion of cases have shown that the child could not be that of the husband. Not so long ago a case was tried in the Divorce Court when a girl of a somewhat loose manner of life became pregnant, and persuaded the young man she said was responsible to marry her. The date of the birth of the child was soon enough after the occasion on which she declared he had had intercourse to raise such suspicions in her husband's mind, that coupled with other features of their meeting on this occasion he sued for nullity of marriage. This action was brought under the statutory provision whereby a man may claim nullity if, within a limited period, he can satisfy the court that his wife was pregnant by another man before the marriage and he was ignorant of her condition. On the evidence the court was far from satisfied that the young woman was telling the truth, and eventually agreed to the offer of both parties to submit to a blood test. The result conclusively proved that the husband was not the father, and there was no evidence concerning the unknown father's identity. So the decree sought was granted. As the law stands (section 11 of the Matrimonial Causes Act, 1965) a decree of nullity does not bastardise the child of a voidable marriage, who is held to be legitimate.

The court, however, has no power to order a blood test of a child in most cases unless the parties agree. The Court of Appeal in October 1968 held in a divorce suit that the court cannot order a blood test if the effect of such order might be to bastardise the child. A blood test could only be ordered if it were in the interests of the child. If the test showed that the husband, the appellant, was not the father, it would not help the child to know that he had no identifiable father. In another decision on the same day the same court sanctioned a blood test of a child aged five years in a divorce suit on the ground that the husband might or might not be the father, but if it showed that he was, perhaps he and his parents might take an interest in the child's welfare.

Following a report of the Law Commission on this vexed question, which has led to a number of conflicting court decisions, a Government Bill was introduced with a view to clarifying the situation. The Family Law Reform Act (1969) enacts that the courts should be empowered to order blood tests in all civil cases where the paternity of a child is in issue; no one should be physically compelled to submit to such test, but a refusal would entitle a judge to call upon the person who refused to justify his attitude.

15 Divorce Abroad

In the old Dominions and Colonies which constituted the original British Commonwealth, the English divorce law prevailed, with due deference to those Colonies where local and religious customs called for exceptional treatment.

In Canada the courts grant divorce on various grounds, differing according to the particular province, in eight of the ten provinces. But in Quebec and Newfoundland there is no civil divorce. In Quebec the family relations are more or less subject to the old French law of the Coutume de Paris.

In New Zealand grounds for divorce in addition to those in England also cover three years' separation, either by mutual consent or after a judicial separation; habitual drunkenness by a wife coupled with neglect of household duties; attempted murder or wounding of a spouse after conviction and imprisonment. Wives may claim a separate domicile for the purpose of a petition after separation for three years or more. With a population of about 2,677,000 the ratio of divorce to marriages in New Zealand was in 1966 about one to eleven.

In Australia a Matrimonial Causes Act came into operation in 1961 which made domicile in any part of the federation the test for jurisdiction instead of the domicile being limited as heretofore to each State. Apart from one marked alteration the grounds of divorce approximated to the English law, subject to certain extra grounds like those in New Zealand. The change made, often invoked as a model by the promoters of the Divorce Reform Act, 1969 in England, was the new ground of five years' separation, which would enable either spouse to claim a divorce. If one of them had been guilty of a matrimonial offence that would not debar him or her from a decree, unless the court found it too harsh and oppressive to the other, in the circumstances.

Australian judges have taken conflicting views of this latter formula in regard to unoffending spouses against whom the other parties, themselves the offenders, have brought divorce suits. Up to 1966 the most common grounds alleged in divorce suits continued to be adultery and desertion, the fresh ground of five years' separation being set up in a small minority of cases. With a population of some 12 million the ratio of divorces to marriages in Australia in 1966 was nearly one to ten.

With the rise of the Holy Roman Empire, comprising most of Western Europe, but excluding Scandinavia, the canon law prevailed. Thus marriage was in theory indissoluble except by the death of a spouse, as already described in Chapter 2. The canon law with regard to divorce is still operated in those countries of Europe in which the Roman Catholic Church preserves its ancient powers and ecclesiastical jurisdiction, with the Sacra Rota in Rome as the supreme court of appeal. But the Italian legislature has recently passed a limited divorce measure.

FRANCE

In France after various changes arising out of the Revolution at the end of the eighteenth century and the Code Napoléon (see Chapter 8), and the abolition of divorce *a vinculo* following the return of the Bourbon monarchs, various laws were passed from 1889 permitting divorce on certain grounds. These are:

1. adultery by either spouse;

2. violence (*excès*) or cruelty (*sévices*);

3. *injures graves,* i.e. allegations reflecting on the honour or reputation, and unjustifiable refusal of conjugal relations and habitual drunkenness;

4. *peine afflictive et infamante*, i.e. conduct involving imprisonment for certain offences.

If spouses separated for three years continuously and refused reconciliation, either could obtain a divorce on application to the court. Press reports of divorce proceedings are forbidden.

The most common ground for divorce in France[1] has been under the heading of *injures graves,* an elastic term. Thus the courts have decreed divorces where the husband repudiated his promise to go through a religious ceremony after the civil marriage ordained by law; or he refused to allow children of the marriage to be baptised; or he insisted against his wife's will on contraceptive methods; or he has been unjustifiably guilty of jealousy and a process of spying on his wife's movements; or he has publicly announced without justification that he will not be liable for her debts. The courts have granted a divorce to a husband on the ground that the wife suppressed the fact of her pregnancy before the marriage. Since the Matrimonial Causes Act 1937 in England this has illogically been made a ground for nullity of marriage, in cases where the woman has had intercourse with some other man. Though in the French system a spouse's impotence is tried under the heading of divorce, the old grounds for nullity of marriage, void *ab initio* or voidable, still prevail. They include lack of parental consent for those who marry under the age of twenty-one; lack of consent by reason of mistake or duress; insanity of a kind which prevents full consent though if the person so afflicted recovers, and no absolute nullity has been decreed, he and he alone can plead in a suit for nullity; prohibited degrees of consanguinity or affinity; bigamy; nonage; and clandestine marriage. All cases of nullity are tried by judges. The most important effect of a putative marriage is that any issue of the union are in French law legitimate, and this applies not only to children born in supposititious wedlock but also to those legitimated by lawful marriage of their parents thereafter.

Judicial separation carries the consequences that the wife has

---

[1] Sir Maurice Amos, Quain Professor, and F. P. Walton, *Introduction to French Law*, Clarendon Press, 1935.

all the civil rights of a single woman, and she is entitled to her own property by a process of *séparation des biens,* and the other spouse loses any right of succession to her estate.

How far a French judgment of divorce or judicial separation between aliens, or if one of them is an alien, will produce the effects mentioned above depends on the complex rules of private international law, best studied in the textbooks on that subject. In general if one spouse is a French national and the other an alien, French law will be applied to the former, and foreign law to the latter, but if there be an irreconcilable conflict between the two laws, the French law prevails.

After the world war of 1939–45 there was as in other countries a great rush of people to the French divorce courts. The peak was 57,400 decrees in 1947, reduced to 47,000 and 32,000 respectively in the next two years. The figure of divorces in 1965 was close on 29,000 and in 1966 a little over 28,000. The annual average of marriages remained more or less constant at 342,000, showing a ratio of one divorce to twelve marriages.

WESTERN GERMANY

In the Federal Republic of Germany, the post-war civil code virtually re-enacts Law No. 16 of the Allied Control Commission in 1946, which was based on the former German Civil Code of 1900. The minimum age for marriage, which in all cases is civil at the equivalent of a registrar's office, is twenty-one years for a male and for a female not before the completion of her seventeenth year, subject to certain exemptions in the case of earlier ages. Parental consent to marriage is the general rule. The usual limitations of consanguinity and affinity apply (though not quite the same as in England) as well as the various forms of lack of consent. Monogamy is the rule.

If a person is divorced for adultery he or she is debarred from marrying the paramour, but as many divorces are granted on other grounds, this prohibition seldom arises.

Subject to judicial exemptions a woman cannot marry again until after ten months from the date of the dissolution of her former marriage, an old principle laid down in case of children being born during the ten months. If a couple live together for five years after a putative marriage, albeit the ceremony is invalid for lack of form, their marriage is treated as valid, and this rule applies in the case of a marriage normally void by reason of its being celebrated merely for the purpose of enabling the wife to take her husband's name, without conjugal relations following.

A spouse may petition for divorce if the other spouse by reason of a serious violation of marriage duties or disreputable conduct disrupting the foundations of the marriage to such an extent that the restoration of common life in the true conjugal sense cannot be expected; this principle also covers the case where the mental derangement of a spouse makes the continuation of marriage in its true sense impossible. A further ground for divorce is when a spouse is suffering from an incurable or repulsive disease and the other spouse petitions.

Divorce is allowed after separation for three years and if, owing to a deeprooted incurable disruption of marital relations, restoration of conjugal life cannot be expected. In such event either spouse can petition for a divorce, and both may agree to it. Any opposition by a respondent spouse may be disregarded if the continuance of the marriage is not justified on a true assessment of the facts, including the interests of children of the marriage.

Condonation bars a divorce, which, moreover, is not permitted if ten years have elapsed from the date when the ground for divorce arose. Even if no countercharge is made in a divorce suit the joint guilt of the partners must be judicially declared if the respondent is shown to have had a ground for divorce on account of the petitioner's guilt; but if only one of the spouses is found guilty it must be so stated in the judgment. Reasonable provisions for maintenance of spouses and children after divorce are laid down, though not quite on the English model; if a person after divorce marries again the previous spouse is not bound to provide maintenance.

Nullity of marriage is equivalent to the English law, subject to some wider grounds, and the effects are the same as in divorce. Evidence of adultery is on the whole easier to satisfy the court on than in England, and the co-respondent, whether male or female, need not be cited, nor can damages be claimed against an adulterer. The ideological grounds of divorce set up during the Nazi régime have been swept away. Dr Ernst Cohn dealing with the law of domestic relations in Western Germany[1] pointed out that it is comparatively easy to obtain a divorce there without imposing on either party the burden of proving that the other party has committed a matrimonial offence. A wife after divorce has the right to retain her husband's surname, unless she is the guilty party and her husband objects.

The disruption of family life in Germany during the second world war combined with the racial grounds for divorce imposed by the Hitler régime led, as in other belligerent countries, to a vast increase in the number of divorces. They numbered 61,789 in 1939, increased to 75,268 in 1950 in the Federal West German Republic, excluding Berlin. From 1960 to 1962 the average annual number was about 48,900. Fewer divorces occurred in the predominately Roman Catholic region of Western Germany. The following table enables one to indicate the ratio of divorces to marriages in Western Germany, the population in 1966 being about 60 million.

Year	Marriages	Divorces
1960	521,445	48,878
1961	529,786	49,280
1962	530,640	49,521
1964	506,184	55,710
1965	492,128	58,718
1966	484,525	58,730

As the annual number of marriages varies very little the ratio of divorces to marriages was somewhat under one divorce to nine marriages.

ITALY

Hitherto no divorce *a vinculo* in Italy has been allowed, and the annual average in three recent years of so-called divorces in

---

[1] *Manual of German Law*, Vol. 1, H.M.S.O., 1950.

statistics probably refers to judicial separations, that is, about 27,000 compared with an annual average of 128,760 marriages. The figure of sentences of nullity does not appear in the statistics. Though the Italian ecclesiastical courts do not recognise divorces relating to Italian nationals, yet if an alien marries in Italy and obtains a divorce in another country such decree, subject to certain conditions, may be enforceable in Italy in special proceedings. In November 1967 a commission of the Chamber of Deputies approved by the narrow margin of 21 votes to 20 a Bill permitting civil divorce on the usual grounds as in France. The proposal was strongly opposed by the Vatican authorities and has made no progress.

In Eire, Spain and Portugal there is no divorce *a vinculo,* though in Portugal divorce may be granted to non-Catholic spouses. For Spain no figures of decrees of judicial separation are available and in Portugal the figure is under 700, probably mostly judicial separations, for 74,000 marriages.

EIRE

The 1937 constitution of Eire (the independent Republic of Southern Ireland) laid it down that no law should be enacted providing for the grant of a dissolution of marriage, and no such law has been enacted. The result is that the Roman canon law prevails, and that decrees of divorce granted by other states are not recognised in Eire. As the constitution provided: 'The State recognises the special position of the Holy Catholic Apostolic and Roman Church as the guardian of the Faith professed by the great majority of the citizens.' So that it would be necessary for an Eire husband to change his domicile to Northern Ireland, where the divorce law is practically the same as in England, or to Great Britain, before he could obtain a divorce, and even then it would seem that such divorce would not be recognised in Eire. Incidentally in Eire the old common law for age at marriage remains, fourteen years for a male and twelve for a female, but despite this in fact the average age of marriage in Eire is one of the highest in the world.

SCANDINAVIA

In the Scandinavian countries and in Holland the usual matrimonial offences afford grounds for divorce, and in the alternative marriage may be dissolved by mutual consent after specific periods of separation.

With a population of 7,843,000 in Sweden, marriages numbered 61,000 in 1966, more or less a constant figure, and the divorces approximately totalled 10,300, showing a ratio of a little over one divorce to six marriages. In Norway with a population of about 3,770,000 in 1966 the equivalent ratio was about one divorce to eight marriages. In Denmark with a population of 4,767,000 the equivalent ratio was somewhat more than one divorce to six marriages.

Whether or not the frequency and ease of divorce in Sweden with the inevitable break-up of families and the making of fresh unions is a harbinger of general social corruption only time will tell. But the freedom of sexual indulgence in that country from the age of puberty, with little or no sense of shame, is a feature of life. Moreover, women have developed a degree of individuality and of equality with men, at any rate in the upper classes, that may well affect the divorce rate. In 1966 there appeared in bulletins of the British National Marriage Guidance Council an instructive series of articles by D. L. Howard, a sociologist, on this aspect of life in Sweden, in which incidentally he wrote that twenty-five per cent of live children born in Iceland are illegitimate, adding: 'The vice, the violence, the dissipation which moralists might predict does not exist or is yet to come.'

AUSTRIA, BELGIUM, SWITZERLAND

Looking at the smaller Western countries the divorce law in Austria and Belgium is very much the same as in Western Germany. In Austria with a population of about 7,200,000, marriages numbered 55,684 in 1966 and divorces 8,643; the ratio was in the neighbourhood of one divorce to seven marriages. In Belgium with a population of some 10,000,000 the ratio worked out at about one divorce to twelve marriages. In Switzerland with a population of about 5,400,000 the ratio is about one divorce to nine marriages.

All three countries contain a considerable Roman Catholic element.

UNION OF SOVIET SOCIALIST REPUBLICS

In Russia after the Revolution spouses could divorce each other by mutual consent or on the application of one spouse only, no questions asked, just a matter for registration. This led to such social chaos that under the 1936 constitution a decree directed that both spouses should state their consent to a divorce at the registration office. That not sufficing to quell the rising volume of divorce, the Presidium in July 1944 passed a new law, 'with a view to increasing financial aid to pregnant women, married mothers with many children and unmarried mothers and to encouraging large families'. Maternity grants to wives were to be provided on the basis of 400 roubles on the birth of a third child, 1,300 roubles on the birth of a fourth child, and progressively until a tenth child was born, with a grant of 5,000 roubles. Monthly grants were also made varying from 80 to 300 roubles. Smaller grants were decreed for unmarried mothers. If a wife brought up five children or more she was to be awarded a Motherhood Medal, and with ten children she was entitled to a Heroine Medal.

Divorce procedure became less easy under this decree, with applications costing 100 roubles and having to set out motives for the breakdown, public notices being given, and hearings in open court, unless a closed court was ordered. The People's Court had to inquire into the causes of the matrimonial rift, and advise reconciliation. There was a right of appeal to a higher court. In some cases the court refused a divorce, e.g. for allegations that the wife did not cook or do the washing, and where the husband set up his own adultery or where adultery had been condoned. If a wife was barren the husband could claim a divorce. In the late 'fifties most divorce applications, however, to which the parties agreed, were granted, and the ratio of divorces to marriages was reported at one to ten.

Nevertheless by 1966 the divorce procedure had become easier, the ground being the breakdown of marriage on the joint asseveration of the spouses. The court carried out only a perfunctory inquisition into the facts and causes, as illustrated in a detailed report of a case in Moscow People's Court published in *The Sunday Times Magazine* of 28 May 1967. The ground for dissolution of a marriage dated 7 September 1963 was loss of mutual respect and trust, and the cessation of conjugal life in February 1966. The trial lasted eight minutes. Both spouses said they had outlived their interest in each other, and the divorce was decreed.

A month later in the same court a young actress was the applicant. In reply to the judge she repeated several times that her reason for requesting a divorce was that she did not love her husband any more and did not want to live with him any longer. The judge continued probing but failed to produce any better reason, except that there was not another man. The young husband, an actor, said he did not object to the divorce, and in ten minutes the decree was granted, on the basis of what might be styled the irretrievable breakdown of the marriage. The couple go out of court together apparently the best of friends. It cost the husband £28.

On 27 June 1968 the Supreme Soviet adopted new principles with regard to marriage and family law, and in consequence the Presidium passed a decree laying down the procedure which became effective on 1 October 1968.[1] Hitherto the system had been general throughout Russia, with minor differences in some of the Republics which constitute the Russian state. It would appear that the new decree more or less revives the easier system of divorce prevailing before 1944. Divorce may be obtained either by a judicial decision when the case is contested, or by the local agencies for registration of documents pertaining to civil status. The marriage can be dissolved on the application of one spouse or both.

If there are no minor children (under eighteen years of age) and they mutually consent to divorce, the marriage is dissolved at the registration office, without court proceedings. The decrees are issued to the spouses three months from the date of their application. The same procedure applies to divorces of persons who have been legally declared as absent with unknown whereabouts, or

[1] The author is indebted to Professor Lapenna, of the London School of Economics, for the details of this law.

incompetent because of mental illness, or have been sentenced to imprisonment for not less than three years for committing a crime. If there is a dispute on any of these questions the marriage may be dissolved by court decision but steps must first be taken to reconcile the spouses.

The age of marriage is not less than eighteen years, but this may be lowered in any Republic by legislation to sixteen years or more. The grounds of divorce are left to the discretion of the court on the basis of a single general rule that a marriage may be dissolved if the court finds that the spouses' continued cohabitation and preservation of the family becomes impossible (Article 14). Thus the present legislation in this respect is practically identical with the former. The most common grounds of divorce were (1) adultery 'contrary to communist morality' (whatever that might mean in a particular case); (2) actual separation over a long period; (3) refusal to continue marital life; (4) repeated drunkenness; (5) major differences in personal culture and education. The chief innovation was divorce by consent.

Statistics of marriages and divorces in the U.S.S.R. are not available, but in December 1967 it was reported from Moscow that in 1965 the rate of divorces to marriages was one to five, and in one district near the capital one to four, drunkenness being the main cause. In November 1968 the official divorce rate was reported to have increased to one divorce for four marriages, and in some districts one divorce to two marriages. To render marriages more durable it was planned that a six months' engagement should precede espousal, and banns be published six months before the ceremony, always civil. A Soviet teacher ventured to assert that the soaring divorce rate with broken homes produced hooliganism, drunkenness and other social ills. On the face of it the 1968 legislation does not appear to promise better things for the stability of family life.

Similarly in Poland, Hungary and Czechoslovakia the only ground of judicial divorce is the breakdown of the marriage, as alleged by the parties without the need of independent corroboration if they are agreed. The ratio of divorce to marriages in Czechoslovakia is a little over one to five.

136

THE UNITED STATES

In the British colonies of North America before their independence in the eighteenth century the only method of divorce was by the Act of the legislative assembly of a particular state, just as in England it required a private Act of Parliament. Differing in racial origin and social customs grounds of divorce in the various states also differ, though on the whole the system originating in England was adopted, the grounds varying from adultery and desertion to incompatibility and separation of spouses for a statutory period. Cruelty is a ground for divorce in most of the states, the broad principle being that the courts may find it where a spouse by inhuman treatment renders the continuance of married life intolerable. Habitual drunkenness is a ground also in most states, and persistent refusal of marital intercourse in about half of the states. Insanity at the time of marriage ranks for divorce rather than annulment, but under this heading the courts have recognised grounds unknown in English law, for example, a divorce in the New York State Court of Appeal in 1965 for an American wife on the ground that her husband suppressed the fact that he had been a Nazi army officer. Even in 1945 an eminent American judge in the famous case of *Williams* v. *North Carolina* emphasised the fact that divorce affected personal rights of the greatest significance and moreover touched basic interests of society.[1]

Everyone has become aware of the divorce mart in the state of Nevada, to which people resort who are not domiciled there, but in which a nominal residence of six weeks enables the court to exercise jurisdiction in divorce. It has been stated that as a result the second biggest business in that state, gambling being the biggest, is that pertaining to quick weddings after divorce. In 1961 nearly 30,000 weddings took place in Las Vegas (with a population of 80,000), on the payment of appropriate fees. Yet this type of divorce and speedy marriage thereafter constitutes only a small proportion of divorces in the U.S.A., the vast majority being granted to people married and domiciled in the states whose courts hear the cases.

[1] Many of these facts are borrowed from the *Encyclopaedia Britannica*.

As in other belligerent countries the effect of the second world war was to send up the number of divorces throughout the U.S.A. to 610,000, but in 1955 the number fell to 377,000, the four years 1956–59 showing an annual average of 381,500. In 1966 with marriages totalling 1,844,000 and divorces 494,000 the ratio of divorces to marriages reached nearly as much as one to four.

MEXICO

Mexico has been in the limelight for years past owing to the ease with which its courts grant divorce decrees, picturesquely got up with coloured ribbons, to all and sundry wherever they come from at an appropriate fee. Foreigners resort to the Mexican courts when they cannot obtain divorces in the countries of their domicile or habitual residence. Strangely enough the New York courts recognise some of these divorces if the applicants have an original domicile in New York State, but the English courts are stricter, as in the case of *Mountbatten* v. *Mountbatten* (Lord Milfordhaven) reported in Law Reports (1959) p. 43.

JEWISH LAW OF DIVORCE

Only a Jewish husband can in theory obtain a divorce, there being no mutual right on the part of a wife. This is still the Jewish law in the Republic of Israel, but in practice he has to show the rabbinical court good cause. If on the other hand a Jewish wife wants a divorce she puts her case to the court, and if it seems just pressure is put on the husband to administer a *ghet* to the wife, on which the court dissolves the marriage on the ground of the husband's adultery or by mutual consent or other grounds. If the parties are not domiciled in Israel such divorces are not recognised in English law, but may be in some other countries such as Egypt in which the jurisdiction of the rabbinical courts is exercised.

JAPAN

In Japan the grounds of divorce have been very wide for many years including those well established in England hitherto and also incompatibility. But in 1949 special family courts were set up for conciliation or on failure thereof divorce by mutual consent on arranged terms. These courts exercised a different procedure in contested cases. Equality of the sexes was recognised, and in sixteen years some 5,500,000 cases were heard by the family courts. Private international law governing the legal relations between husband and wife has shown marked developments in recent years, and in 1961 the court refused to recognise a divorce granted in Nevada, U.S.A., to a Japanese husband on the ground of three years' separation, and granted the Japanese wife a divorce.

CHINA

In communist China monogamy was enacted for marriage. Divorce might be decreed for adultery or on the mutual consent of the parties. The easy divorce common in the time of the old Chinese Empire and even before has given way to more legalist methods. No more can a man divorce his wife for serving her mother-in-law with badly stewed prunes as a certain Patron Saint of Filial Piety did in ancient days.

SOUTH AFRICA

Though no statistics of divorces in the Republic of South Africa are given in the *Statesmen's Yearbook*, with a white population of some 3,480,000 in 1966 there were 35,500 marriages. In February 1968 the *Daily Telegraph* correspondent in Cape Town reported that almost four out of ten marriages were breaking down within a year. This caused the appointment by the Government of a commission of inquiry. A judge of the Cape Town Supreme Court said that South African Courts were becoming mere machines for divorce. The most common ground for divorce in the Republic is desertion, with adultery in the second place.

The emergent sovereign countries in Africa which were given their independence by Great Britain have not reached a stage of ordered Government sufficient to provide a code of law for marriage and divorce with so many racial and tribal differences. Only in Kenya has a movement been set on foot to this end. A Commission was appointed in April 1967, with Mr Justice Spry as chairman, to revise the law, having regard to the variety of social and religious customs of matrimony and divorce in that country. In its report the commission opted for customary marriage to be maintained, including polygamy for the Moslems and others, subject to agreement between a man and his first wife that she could insist either on monogamy or the right to choose a second wife for her husband; but the commission thought that for economic reasons polygamy would die. It was recommended that there should be a uniform law of divorce from which it would seem that the Moslem procedure of Talak—divorce by word of mouth repeated three times—would no longer subsist. So far as the English population was concerned the English laws of marriage and divorce would still apply.[1]

[1] Paper by Eugene Cotran, 17 February 1969, under auspices of British Institute of Comparative and International Law.

16 Breakdown of Marriage

During the quarter of a century or so since the end of the second world war, notable changes have taken place in social habits, not least in the development of television which has opened the eyes of millions, old and young, to vast new horizons. New universities have sprung up in which youth is given ample chances of completing their education, thanks to public subsidies. Domestic service has died out except for the rich. Despite the provision of council houses at modest rents, the shortage of housing still remains a serious problem for those with small incomes, intensified recently by a difficulty in obtaining mortgages. Taxation to meet the demands of successive governments has increased enormously. The old cry, 'England is going to the dogs', is heard throughout the land but nevertheless to all seeming Britannia remains prosperous under the Welfare State.

A feature of recent legislation and public administration is the effort made for the welfare of children and people mentally afflicted or deficient. On the other side of the coin is the agitation of groups of university students, most of them maintained by the tax or the rate payer, for a voice in the ruling of colleges and the choice of subjects for study. Many sociologists claim that since the war of 1939–45 children have matured very much earlier than heretofore and are therefore entitled to be given greater responsibilities. But there are many who, though agreeing that children have matured much earlier physically, contend they have not done so mentally.

Be that as it may, it is a fact that the films and television and erotic literature have brought into the open the vagaries of sex far more than was deemed desirable in Victorian or even Edwardian eyes, for both adults and young people. Words concerning sex which were taboo are common form except in polite circles, and call to mind ancient times when vulgar ribaldry was thought nothing of. But so far we have not returned to the habits described by the hero of Mark Twain's *A Yankee at the Court of King Arthur* (1889) who portrayed at a royal palace banquet a scene of rude revels, in which 'men told anecdotes terrific to hear but nobody blushed and the assembly let go a horse-laugh that shook the fortress', the Court ladies included. After all, Chaucer, and Rabelais even more so, only depicted the coarseness of their times.

In fact there is no doubt that in England as in other countries during the last few years a rebellion against authority and old-fashioned principles has developed especially among young people. Whether for good or bad the country is faced with the notion of a permissive society, even reflected in the treatment of grave crime. It is against this background that the growth of domestic disharmony so often leading to divorce has to be considered.

As regards divorce, two schools of thought exist, the one which contends that the fewer marriages are dissolved the better for the family structure, and the other—the individual husband or wife who maintain that if after a three or four years' trial they cannot make a reasonable success of marriage they should be entitled to end it, as was the practice in the pre-Christian era.

In English law in 1968 a divorce could only be sanctioned if one or other of the spouses had committed a matrimonial offence, adultery, cruelty, desertion, or one of less advertised offences of a perverse sort. Most people regard their differences as personal matters which ought not to be brought into the light of day by the publicity which a minority of divorce suits attract. Doubtless sensitive people shrink from going into the witness box to tell judges what has happened in the home or elsewhere to bring about domestic disaster. If they are allowed merely to declare that the marriage has irretrievably broken down, without going into the causes, they will be freed from the fear of publicity. That was partly the basis of the private member's Bill. The question is whether the curtain of silence should be drawn over the wrong-doings of married people that lead to divorce, or whether in order to preserve the principle of the intended lifelong marriage the responsibility for the breakdown should be attributed to the wrongdoer.

The vast majority of divorce suits are undefended, and most of these are not reported in the Press. Judgments in defended suits are sometimes reported, but only in comparatively few, and such judgments are deemed necessary by the court not only to attribute the responsibility for wrongdoing to one spouse or the other, but also to satisfy the Court of Appeal, should there be an appeal, that the judge has considered all the essential evidence. It is true that in a defended suit, as the Bill proposed, the polite euphemism of 'irretrievable breakdown of marriage' would not suffice, if the defendant party alleged such serious matrimonial offences on the part of the other as the court could not ignore.

Let us see how the divorce judges work. Walk into any of the many courts in the Strand where decrees are churned out day after day. In the average undefended suit in which desertion or adultery is pleaded the case is all over in about ten minutes, if the requisite evidence is forthcoming. The petitioner goes into the witness box in a court usually empty except for the judge, officials, and one or two witnesses. The petitioner is treated with courtesy and patience by the judge, who generally says nothing more than pronouncing a decree *nisi*, unless he intervenes to help a nervous petitioner.

If the petitioner has to confess his or her own adultery, which has followed or has not been the cause of the respondent's matrimonial offence, the judge in almost every case exercises his discretion in making a decree. In undefended cases where 'cruelty' is pleaded the evidence often makes it necessary for the court to take double the time to hear the corroboration, but a petitioner receives the same polite treatment from the court. In such a case the evidence may be too flimsy to justify a decree, and then the judge either orders an adjournment for more satisfactory evidence or dismisses the petition.

Cruelty in the Divorce Court has been judicially stretched since that sound judge, Lord Stowell, laid down the criterion in 1790—

143

more concisely put by the House of Lords in *Russell* v. *Russell* (1897) Appeal Cases 395—as conduct such as to have caused danger to life, limb or health, bodily or mental, or as to give rise to a reasonable fear of such danger. With so many judges sitting in divorce, High Court or County Court judges, the interpretation of cruelty by one spouse to another has varied enormously. *Tot homines, quot sententiae,* and the somewhat anaemic formula adopted in the Divorce Reform Act as a substitute—that the respondent has behaved in such a way that the petitioner cannot reasonably be expected to live with the respondent—seems more vague and uncertain than ever. In the past petitions have included charges so frivolous or ridiculous that they throw doubt upon the substance of the case, and judges have had to use their commonsense and knowledge of life in dealing with them.

In many of these cases a conflict develops on questions of maintenance of wives and children and the custody of the latter. When these matters are in dispute they are seldom disposed of at the trial. Wives take out summonses for maintenance which are adjudicated by the court registrars in London and the provinces, subject to the possibility of appeal to a divorce judge. It has been laid down by successive Presidents of the Divorce Division that where a judge is called upon to fix the amount of maintenance it should be for the trial judge, who has heard the evidence, to decide. But the vast number of divorce suits often renders this impracticable, especially in the County Courts in which the judges have other demands on their time than trying divorce suits.

In general the law protecting wives from being left high and dry by their husbands has been strengthened by recent Acts of Parliament, especially in saving them from unjust eviction from the matrimonial home and from the attempt of husbands to so dispose of their property as to leave little or nothing for the wives' maintenance. The Royal Commission on Divorce (1956; Cmd 9678) dealt with the question how far a husband should be ordered to pay maintenance having regard to the fact that so many married women nowadays are employed with salaries or wages. Courts have to take a wife's separate means into account in awarding maintenance.

Lord Denning (then Lord Justice) said in the Court of Appeal.[1]

If a wife does earn, then her earnings must be taken into account; or if she is a young woman with no children, and obviously ought to go out to work in her own interest, but does not, then her potential earning capacity ought to be taken into account; or if she had worked regularly during the married life, and might reasonably be expected to work after the divorce, her potential earnings ought to be taken into account. Except in cases like these it does not as a rule lie in the mouth of a wrong-doing husband to say that she ought to go out to work simply to relieve him from paying maintenance.

Nevertheless experience has shown that in many cases husbands manage to disappear to avoid paying maintenance with the result that their wives, if they have young children to look after, are thrown upon one of the forms of benefit from the Ministry of Social Security for the sustenance of the family. The amount found by the taxpayer for this assistance has reached formidable dimensions.

The Royal Commission also considered that if a wife who had obtained a divorce married again she should cease to have any claim against her divorced husband. The courts have dealt with such a situation by measuring the financial benefit, if any, she derives from her aftertaken husband, against the maintenance which her former husband has been ordered to pay. The Matrimonial Proceedings and Property Bill now nearing the Statute Book provides that a wife who divorces her husband shall no longer be entitled to maintenance from him if she marry another man.

Lord Hodson, the Lord of Appeal, who practised at the Bar and sat as judge for many years in the Divorce Court, referred in a letter to *The Times* on 2 September 1968, to the plight of deserted wives with young children:

The situation of wives will be made worse if the efforts now being

[1] *Rose* v. *Rose* (1951), p. 29.

made for easier divorce are successful. Many of us, who have opposed compulsory divorce after a lapse of time against the will of the deserted wife, have therefore drawn attention to the plight of the wife for whom no adequate provision can be made except out of the taxpayer's pocket. The supporters of the Bill . . . have no remedy to offer except that divorce could be refused in cases where no adequate provision could be made by the husband.

In passing it may be mentioned that this safeguard was modified by a later clause in the Bill to the effect that the financial provision made by the petitioner for the respondent is 'the best that can be made in the circumstances'.

Lord Hodson in his evidence before the Royal Commission on Divorce (1956 Report) had referred to another difficulty arising in divorce where the husband marries again and his wages are such that he cannot maintain both his ex-wife and his new wife, and possibly two lots of children. He pointed out that it was practically impossible for the wife who divorced him to enforce her right to maintenance. There is not enough money to go round. If recourse is made by the ex-wife or the aftertaken wife to the Ministry of Social Security that body has the task of deciding to which woman assistance should be given. In practice, he said, it was easier to enforce maintenance for those with whom the man was living than for those from whom he was parted.

The Lord Chancellor, Lord Gardiner, in supporting this proposal, in an address to the National Marriage Guidance Council at Brighton in May 1967, expressed his personal view thus:

A good divorce law should, when a marriage has irretrievably broken down, enable the empty shell to be destroyed with the maximum fairness and the minimum bitterness. Maintenance of the legal tie of marriage should no longer be regarded as a punishment for the offending spouse, but as a relief for human suffering.

He then referred to the compensating financial provision for the deserted spouse, and the benefits of the conciliation proposals.

Commenting on this view, Mr J. Jackson, Q.C., experienced in divorce proceedings, wrote:

Divorce begets divorce; it is something of a virus . . . The law conditions people's approach to marriage and divorce. People tend to want things that are available. There is a dangerous belief that divorce is a cure for matrimonial unhappiness. 'Bury the marriage and you live again.' It is far from true in many cases; divorce simply results in loneliness, despair and serious financial hardship.

He also raised a point which has often been discussed by those who are anxious to preserve the institution of lifelong marriage. 'Is it too easy to marry?' he wrote.

There is no hardship in making it compulsory for persons to register their intention to marry which can occur with or without a formal engagement, with a compulsory period between the date of registration and the date of marriage. On registration of the intention to marry, both parties should be furnished with a booklet describing in brief, simple terms the responsibilities, financial and otherwise, involved in marriage . . . *Marriage Guidance* should be brought to the attention of parties at the very outset, and not when it is too late for marriage guidance counsellors to be of real assistance.

In passing it should be emphasised that there is a most anomalous distinction between the amounts of Government grants to marriage guidance bodies: £62,625 in 1967, and over £3 million spent by the state in Legal Aid in divorce suits.

Mr Justice Scarman, as chairman of the Law Commission set up to amend or add to present law where deemed advisable, naturally gave his mind to divorce as one of the main problems for reform. In the course of a public lecture at Bristol University in March 1966 he said:

The doctrine of the matrimonial offence requires the petitioner who has offended to pass through the hoop of a discretion at a public hearing, as also it requires that the respondent by admission or by other evidence be found guilty of offence. Yet the distinction in family life between innocence and guilt is often impossible to draw. Most matrimonial offences are merely symptoms, not the disease itself. A true inquiry would concern itself with the breakdown.

He favoured judicial process for divorce being strengthened.

Society's interest in the preservation of family life, and, when it is fragmented by breakdown, in binding up the wounds inflicted upon spouses and children, requires that the tie of marriage should be lawfully dissolved only when these interests are properly safeguarded. Spouses, their judgment distorted by marital unhappiness, cannot be relied upon to put first the objective that society must seek to achieve in its regulation of family life.

Sir Leslie Scarman went on to urge the creation of regional family courts and a Family Division of the High Court to administer the law in matrimonial causes, and that be added to the existing grounds for divorce that of separation on irretrievable breakdown of marriage. He also stressed that it should be the duty of the court to refuse divorce unless there was no reasonable chance of reconciliation, and unless proper arrangements were made for the care of children and financial support of members of the family exposed to risk by the destruction of the family unit.

The Report of the Archbishop's Committee on Divorce appointed in 1964 was issued in 1966 under the title of *Putting Asunder*. It recommended irretrievable breakdown of marriage as the only ground of divorce, but was opposed to divorce by mutual consent as a separate ground.

The Law Commission, under the chairmanship of Sir Leslie Scarman, went closely into the pros and cons of the doctrine of breakdown of marriage, and in its Report in November 1966 entitled *The Field of Choice*, was of the opinion that this might be added as an additional ground to the existing matrimonial offences as grounds. The Commission, however, favoured divorce by

148

mutual consent of the spouses, the consenting parties being the best judges, though critics urged that in the future as now divorce should be subject to an authority independent of the will of the parties, in the interests of the state.

Later the Law Commission and the Archbishops' Committee put their heads together and there arose between them a consensus in favour of breakdown as the only ground of divorce, subject to certain conditions. This was in the view of an important body of opponents an unholy compromise, likely vastly to increase the number of undefended suits, and to weaken the powers of the court against abuse. But the private member's Bill was introduced in 1968 to give effect to this consensus. The Bill passed its second reading, was strenuously opposed in most of its aspects in Committee, and failed to reach the Report stage before the end of the parliamentary session.

The Bill was reintroduced in the next session, the main proposals being:

1. Irretrievable breakdown of marriage the only ground of divorce in future, with the court empowered to consider the chances of reconciliation;

2. Divorce by mutual consent of spouses after two years' separation;

3. After five years' separation divorce against the will of one of the spouses;

4. Existing powers of judges to examine into possibilities of collusion to present a false case to the court, connivance at adultery to be extinguished as a bar to divorce;

5. Provisions for improving safeguards for maintenance of wives.

The clause in the Bill which aroused the keenest opposition was that which would enable one spouse to divorce the other after

L

five years' separation on the ground of irretrievable breakdown of marriage. To an unoffending spouse condemned to a divorce against his or her will this seemed on the face of it an intolerable injustice. In many such cases a husband deserts his wife, guiltless of any matrimonial offence, for a mistress, whom he wants to marry. Generally the wife does divorce him, but if she refused to do so for religious or other reasons it was proposed in the Bill that after five years the husband could divorce her, thus taking advantage of his own wrongdoing.

A fervent appeal was made by promotors of the Bill for sympathy for the illegitimate children born of illicit unions the parties to which could not intermarry because an aggrieved spouse refused to divorce the offending spouse. An extraordinarily large number of such illegitimates was mentioned, on the basis of a statistical hypothesis in a Law Commission Report, who could be legitimated if their parents were free to marry. But Mr Bruce Campbell, Q.C., M.P., suggested in the second reading debate that the way to deal with illegitimate children is to alter the law relating to illegitimacy, and not the divorce laws.

The part played by the matrimonial jurisdiction by magistrates, with their power of judicial separation, adds heavily to the problem of broken marriages, the orders made every year for maintenance of wives and children and the custody of the latter amounting to many thousands a year.

The law of nullity of marriage is being considered by the Law Commission. It does not present such a grave problem as the law of divorce, inasmuch as the average annual number of decrees *nisi* of nullity for the seven years 1961–66 was only 675. But in a working paper issued in 1967 the Law Commission expressed the view that the law was not wholly clear or satisfactory. Several possible changes were discussed, such as three years being substituted for one year from the date of marriage during which a spouse might impeach the marriage on grounds of nullity first set out in the Matrimonial Causes Act 1937; the abolition of parental consent for marriage after the age of eighteen which was advocated in Mr Justice Latey's Age of Majority Report; no ratification of a marriage where either party was under sixteen years of age; children of spouses should be separately represented in suits where the marriage is to be void *ab initio*; approbation of a voidable marriage should be a bar to the suit. So far no definite recommendations have been made in the form of a Parliamentary measure.

In this connection the somewhat confusing situation on jurisdiction still remains to be examined. Epilepsy as a ground for nullity, first laid down in the Matrimonial Causes Act 1937, has been questioned by the medical profession.

17 Passing of the Bill

Mr Leo Abse, M.P., the prime mover of the Divorce Reform Bill, on the second reading in February 1968, made the following points:

1. The family is becoming more democratic, more egalitarian. It is becoming a place where money is shared, where the house may be shared jointly, where the mortgage is paid for by both; where, because of the rising female activity rate in Britain, it inevitably means that the family unit is more of a coalition.

2. It is not something vague and indefinite that the judges must decide when considering whether or not a marriage has irretrievably broken down. We are saying in clause 2(1) that 'the petitioner satisfies the court of one or more of the following facts'. The judges can adjudicate on the facts not on some vague concept . . . whether or not, on the evidence before them, the parties have been apart for two or five years, as the case may be. We are by no means divesting themselves of what is to be regarded as declared acknowledgement that a marriage has broken down.

3. It must surely be an advance if we are able to say that two people end their marriage in dignity after they have been apart for two years because they do not want to acclaim to the world the cruelty of one side or the adultery of the other. Why do some want to have emblazoned abroad and publicly declared that one

party is innocent and one party guilty? . . . Since 30 per cent of those who go for divorce on the ground of the guilt of the other side are admitting that they have committed adultery. What sort of humbug is it that says that we must stand on an old divorce law which demands that men and women must be found innocent or guilty? . . . We can get rid of this public washing of dirty linen which takes place in long drawn-out cruelty cases, so that a man can allow a divorce to go through on the ground of marriage breakdown.

He went into details concerning the proposed financial safeguards for wives divorced against their will under the five years' separation clause, and in the latter debates in Standing Committee frequently intervened to oppose amendments put forward to clarify the Bill and introduce safeguards against abuse.

On an amendment to the effect that the court should be satisfied that the causes of the breakdown should be sufficient to justify a decree of divorce, Mr Abse said:

4. It could be regarded as a 'Nosey Parker's Charter', because it would seriously undermine the enlargement of the right to privacy and personal choice which we are deliberately creating in the Bill. Is it not really overwhelming arrogance on our part for us to say to a couple, already apart for two years, both adamantly declaring their marriage is dead, that the man in the Strand knows best? [Official Report, 15 May 1968.]

On the five years' separation clause he said:

5. One cannot say that it is an enhancement of the respect for marriage that there are tens of thousands of men and women desperately anxious to regularise their position in the community who are unable to do so . . . It is because I am not prepared to accept what I regard as a novelettish approach to the problem that I do not believe that the passing of this provision will in any way precipitate more breakdowns in marriage. It will make for more marriages. People will be able to marry as a consequence

of being able to obtain a death certificate in respect of a marriage already long since dead. [Official Report, 22 May 1968.]

The Bill passed its second reading in the Commons by 159 votes to 63.

The Bill having lapsed for lack of time in the 1967–68 session, it was reintroduced, subject to the deletion of clause 4 providing for the refusal of a decree if the petitioner attempted to deceive the Court. In the further second reading debate in the House of Commons, Mr Abse again wholeheartedly championed the Bill. He said about the doctrine of a matrimonial offence being the ground for divorce:

6. Because guilt has to be proved, our divorce courts are replete with charades that bring law and the institution of marriage into disrepute. It is because of this wretched doctrine that the perjuries, the rigged adulteries and the faked desertions masking the mutuality of the original parting we have the puffed-up allegations of cruelty and the publicised descretion statements, which this Bill gets rid of ... Because of the doctrine of the matrimonial offence, judges and lawyers are reduced to the rôle of scavengers having to scrape round for the worst obscenities they can find within a married life, and, within the present accusatorial system, hurling all their wretched findings across the courtroom.

The declared substitution in the Bill of the doctrine of matrimonial breakdown means that attention can be rivetted not upon punishment, not upon the public branding of alleged sinners, but on the question whether the marriage can be healed, and if, lamentably, it cannot be healed, then at least it can be ended by the parties, who, after being apart for two years, could almost privately, with dignity and without public recrimination, see the end of their lamentably dead marriage. 'Only if we emancipate ourselves from the doctrine of the matrimonial offence can we begin to move forward to considerations of how courts and lawyers can be deployed as marriage menders and not as marriage breakers.' (Official Report, 17 December 1968.)

It would be wearisome for the reader to set out at length the many objections to the principles and form of the Bill raised by its opponents, prominent among whom were the following M.P.s: Sir Lionel Heald, Q.C., the Hon. Richard Wood, Dame Irene Ward, Mr Ian Percival, Q.C., Mr Marcus Worsley and Mr Bruce Campbell, Q.C., Mr John Biggs-Davison, M.P. and Mr Doughty, Q.C., but as the public do not read the Hansard Reports, the main objections may be put thus:

1. Irretrievable breakdown of marriage is an abstract term. In the case of an undefended petition for divorce on the ground of separation for two years or more all that the petitioner has to say to the judge is that the spouses cannot get on together, and the respondent does not oppose the suit. The judge, as the Bill proposed, has no power of inquisition, and must make a rubber-stamp decree, without hearing any evidence but that of the petitioner.

2. Such ugly facts as connivance at adultery, or collusion by way of suppression of the real facts, are brushed aside, the former powers of the court in those respects being repealed. It is a public fallacy that most undefended divorce suits hitherto have been collusive. They are based on proved matrimonial offences.

3. By authorising one spouse to divorce the other against the latter's will after five years' separation Parliament will have instituted for the first time the principle that a person may take advantage of his or her own wrong. In any event the number of such petitions would be minute compared with the vast volume of petitions.

4. The burden of proof is not on the petitioner to satisfy the court that the marriage has irretrievably broken down, but on the respondent, who for divers reasons may not wish to take any part in the case. If of course the respondent defends, he or she may show good cause that it is the petitioner's own wrongdoing which broke down the marriage, but even then the court may be compelled to find, as the Bill stands, that such defence is of no avail, because the breakdown of the marriage is irretrievable.

5. The Bill was silent on the interests of children likely to be seriously affected by the divorce of their parents, existing provisions in the Matrimonial Causes Act 1965 not being adequate in view of the changes proposed in the Bill.

6. The Law Commission was often invoked by promoters of the Bill in support of the doctrine of irretrievable breakdown, as the single ground, with matrimonial offences such as adultery, desertion and gross ill-treatment as 'guide lines'; but Sir Leslie Scarman, chairman of the Commission, had publicly expressed his own view that this doctrine should only be treated as an additional ground of divorce to the old-established matrimonial offence.

7. To grant divorces after two years' separation would be to encourage young people to enter into 'trial' marriages, and would undoubtedly increase the existing number of divorces, already running at nearly 50,000 a year. It is an unfortunate fact that far too many marriages of very young people end in the Divorce Court within four or five years, and the reduction to eighteen years for parental consent following Mr. Justice Latey's Report on the Age of Majority now the law under the Family Law Reform Act, 1969, may swell the number.

8. The proposed financial protection for wives deserted by their husbands who may divorce them against their will is allusory in respect of people of small means. In any event such legislation should be postponed pending the promised Government Bill covering the whole question of maintenance and matrimonial property, a point stressed by Sir Lionel Heald in debate and in a letter to *The Times* (11 March 1969). The plea for postponement till better protection of wives' interests is enacted, was eventually granted and the Matrimonial Proceedings and Property Bill was introduced by the Government.

All these points were raised by critics of the Divorce Reform

Bill in the House of Commons Standing Committee and rejected by a majority.

On the larger question, whether or not the main object of the Bill was justified, Mr W. A. Wilkins, M.P. for Bristol South, warned colleagues in the House that they would have a rude awakening at future elections if they persisted in the Bill, inasmuch as women in general and important married women's associations in particular throughout the country had expressed their abhorrence. During the debates the views of many such associations had been canvassed, almost entirely hostile to the proposal for divorce after five years' separation, against an unoffending spouse.

The progress of the Bill on its reintroduction followed the pattern of the previous debate, with more or less the same arguments for and against. In December 1968 the Bill again passed its second reading in the Commons by 183 votes to 106. It was announced on behalf of the Government that the latter was neutral, although in fact the Bill was backed by the Law Commission.

One supporter of the Bill in the Standing Committee (Official Report, 5 March 1969) maintained that the interests of the children must come second to those of their parents in divorce proceedings. But opponents moved amendments to the effect that if there are any children of the marriage under sixteen years of age the court will grant a decree only if satisfied that it is clearly in the child's interest to do so.

On this point Mr Bruce Campbell, M.P., in support of one such amendment, said:

This Bill is said to have as one of its objects the encouraging of reconciliation between spouses. There is no doubt that children keep a great many marriages together. Most people are decent people, and even if they are tired of the marriage and would perhaps like to make their lives in future with other partners will weigh up the interests of their children. There must be many husbands still living with wives, and wives with husbands who are doing so not because they want to do so, but because,

M

having children, they say: 'I have made my bed and now I shall lie on it', and they make the best of their marriages in the children's interests. Often happily it turns out to be a very good best, and marriages which might easily have gone on the rocks, and which have been saved by the children often turn out to be quite happy marriages. [Official report, 5 March 1969.]

The amendment was rejected by a majority of eight to five votes. Mr Bruce Campbell moved an amendment to the clause enabling a spouse to divorce the other after five years' separation so that it should not be retrospective, and those who had already married on the basis of a lifelong union should not be affected. One speaker quoted the words of the Archbishop of Canterbury in an article in the *Sunday Times* in February 1968, when the Bill was first introduced: 'Under the new proposal the initiative [in petitioning] can be taken by the unfaithful spouse. This would make intervention in a marriage more attractive to an adventurer or adventuress.' The amendment was rejected by 130 votes to 30.

Much of the rest of the debate, which went on throughout the night until the next afternoon, revolved over the question of religious scruples against divorce. The proposal for divorce after five years' separation was vehemently opposed time after time, and the inadequacy of the provisions for financial safeguards of unoffending married women divorced against their will loomed large in the debate. The Bill was given a Third Reading by 109 votes to 55, a total of 164 members registering their votes.

Lord Stow Hill (formerly Sir Frank Soskice, Attorney-General) moved the Second Reading of the Bill in the House of Lords on 30 June 1969, in a speech of studied moderation but pressing hard in favour of the measure as it stood. The most heated controversy was over the clause for allowing a divorce, possibly against the will of a deserted spouse, after five years' separation. The most convincing critics were Baroness Summerskill and Lord Reid, the Law Lord.

Lady Summerskill claimed that the far-reaching social importance of the Bill had not been recognised. Only a quarter of the

600 M.P.s had voted for or against the Bill. This was certainly not the will of the inarticulate women and children who might be the victims of the Bill. She quoted the view of the 1955 Royal Commission on Divorce:

To vest in a husband or wife the right to divorce a spouse who had committed no recognised matrimonial offence and who did not want a divorce would result in grave injustice. It would allow a man who had committed adultery or had been cruel to his wife to leave her and subsequently to divorce her against her will. This would violate a principle which has long been established in the law that a man shall not be allowed to take advantage of his own wrong.

Lord Reid said that he was suspicious of any proposal to advance the public good by doing injustice to individuals. He was doubtful about getting rid of connivance and condonation and a number of other things. As to divorce after two years' separation he urged that the respondent should give his or her consent instead of merely not objecting. He was opposed to the five years' separation clause because of its injustice: they had to consider the discarded wife who was completely blameless. The right thing to do was to postpone this clause, if adopted, until the promised Bill for financial protection of deserted wives was passed.

Lord Sandford, also opposing the five years' separation clause, commented on the inconsistency of £30 million being spent from public funds on children in care, most of whom came from broken families, and a further £30 million on supplementary benefit for unmarried mothers and deserted and divorced wives, as compared with the £100,000 granted to the marriage guidance agencies.

The Lord Chancellor defended the Government's action in allowing time for the Bill though neutral as to its contents. He invoked the examples of New Zealand and Australia in allowing divorce after five years' separation. The Archbishop of Canterbury criticised blemishes in the Bill and decided that he could not vote for it.

After a number of other speeches for or against the Bill or certain aspects of it—notably Baroness Gaitskell, the Bishop of Exeter, Lord Denning, Master of the Rolls, and Lord Goodman, for; Lord Longford and Lord Hodson, Law Lord, against, the House of Lords accorded the Bill a Second Reading by 122 votes to 34.

In the subsequent Committee stage the same pattern followed as in the Commons Committee, the rejection of important amendments, with one notable exception. By 65 to 61 votes the House resolved that divorce by mutual consent should really be by consent, positively expressed by the respondent, instead of the weaker formula of not objecting. On the Report stage an amendment was agreed to whereby the Act will not come into force till 1 January 1971. Lord Dilhorne, the ex-Lord Chancellor, took an active part in the debates, in opposition to some aspects of the Bill.

18 Reflections

Turning to a final review of this Act, initiated not with Government responsibility but through the persistence of a small number of M.P.s, let us look at the kernel of the matter. Much was made by the leading champion of the Bill for the need of quiet semi-private divorces with no fault being attributed to either party, and no recriminations in court. Some people think that this would be a further sop to the permissive society which has developed so widely since the last war. Thus under the Bill 'cruelty' as a ground for divorce under that offensive name should be abolished. Instead Parliament substituted the words, 'such conduct by a spouse as makes it intolerable for the petitioner to continue to live with the respondent'. Insomuch as for years past divorce judges have been dealing with such cases of alleged cruelty more or less according to the new formula here is a verbal distinction without a difference.

Then what about the co-respondent? It is true that in defended divorce suits he may be cited and damages claimed against him as in existing law. But the vast majority of cases are undefended and unreported. Supposing the case of a man petitioning for divorce on the ground of irretrievable breakdown of marriage after two years' separation is prevailed on not to cite his wife's lover. He says nothing about her adultery. She does not appear. The petitioner gets his decree. It may be said that this already happens in undefended cases, but the petitioner has to prove some matrimonial offence to the satisfaction of the judge.

Lady Summerskill, addressing an audience of women about the Bill, described it when first introduced as a 'Casanova's Charter' for the wealthy man with a roving eye. (*Daily Telegraph*, 24 January 1968). She said that the compulsory divorce of an innocent spouse opened the door to the divorce of the chronic sick together with those who had become incompatible through no fault of their own.

One aspect of the measure in particular puzzled a good many, the policy of putting the cart before the horse, i.e. granting a decree by the mutual consent of the spouses. In order that the marriage might be dissolved with a minimum of discomfort to the spouses, any hidden cause concerning the conduct of one party or the other would be left until questions of maintenance or custody of children had to be dealt with. Then, and not until then, would the mutual conduct of the parties be tried by the court.

On the other hand Mr Justice Ormrod, well versed in divorce practice both as counsel and Judge, has written: 'On the face of it the Bill looks like a far-reaching measure of reform, and, if its provisions are compared section by section with the Matrimonial Causes Act, 1965, it is easy to demonstrate the radical changes introduced by the new measure. But if one compares its proposals with the actual present practice of the Court in its divorce jurisdiction, the changes, real though some are, become less significant.'[1] He referred to the fact that what are known as matrimonial offences would apparently still play an important part under the Bill in adjudication by the Court.

The Government's main reason for passing the Matrimonial Causes Act 1967, conferring jurisdiction for the first time in England on the county courts instead of High Court judges, was that there would be a saving of £400,000 on the Legal Aid Fund. Quite apart from doubts expressed that there would be any such saving, it has been estimated by an advisory committee of the Lord Chancellor that the Divorce Reform Bill would cost the Fund between £300,000 and £400,000. This does not take

---

[1] 'The Divorce Law Reform Bill', *Bulletin of the National Marriage Guidance Council*.

into account a possibly equivalent sum payable in supplementary assistance to destitute wives owing to the expected increase in the number of divorces.

There is a conflict of opinion in the Church with regard to divorce nowadays.[1] Though most of the clergy cling to the ideal of lifelong marriage, they realise, first, that state laws are supreme, and, secondly, that divorce should be looked upon as a safety valve in exceptional cases. Dr Mortimer, Bishop of Exeter, who was the chairman of the Archbishop's Committee that produced the Report, *Putting Asunder*, has asserted that in the modern world divorce has lost its stigma. In a debate in the House of Lords on divorce law reform (Official Report, Vol. 278, col. 247) the Bishop suggested that a delay between a divorce and a second marriage was highly desirable. In his experience marriages after divorce which had proved most stable were those almost invariably contracted some time after the divorce and having nothing to do with the obtaining of the divorce.

It is not known whether or not there is any considerable body of opinion in the country in favour of the Bill. This measure with all its consequences to the structure of society has not been put to the country. A variety of personal experiences about the problems of broken marriage and divorce was published by the *Guardian* in 1968.[2] In an introduction a woman writer, referring to the situation arising if one spouse 'through spite or religious conviction refused a divorce to the other', said that the result was often a subsequent 'bigamous common law marriage' (incidentally a polite phrase often used in the House of Commons). The writer added: 'There are reckoned to be some 180,000 children of stable illicit unions.' This figure, cited in support of the five years' separation divorce in the Bill is of doubtful origin. By what statistical method was it produced? Apparently the figure originated in paragraph 36 of the Law Commission's Report, *Field of Choice*,[3] dealing with the illegitimate progeny of illicit unions.

[1] *What the Bishops have said about Marriage*, S.P.C.K., 1968; Canon A. R. Winnett, *The Church and Divorce*, Mowbray, 1968.
[2] *Marriage and Divorce*, ed. Christopher Macy, Pemberton, 1969.
[3] Cmnd 3123, 1967.

In the fifteen years up to 1964 inclusive there were 607,000 live illegitimate births in England and Wales. Miss V. Wimperis in her book *The Unmarried Mother and her Child* (Allen and Unwin, 1960) estimated that 40 per cent of these could not be legitimated as the law stands. The Law Commission reduced this estimate to 30 per cent, bringing the total to 182,000. Thus the figure of 180,000, but what has this to do with the comparatively small number of people living together in illicit unions whose spouses have declined to divorce them? These constitute a minute minority and any expert in divorce law would be able to advise that in some of these cases when one spouse has left the other because of the latter's persistent and overbearing behaviour it is the other spouse who has been guilty of constructive desertion. In other words the apparently deserting spouse might divorce the other under the existing law.

If the Bill becomes law what will be the position of divorce judges? It will be fairly easy if the petitioner relies on one of the 'guide lines' set out in clause 2(1)(*b*) and (*c*)—intolerable behaviour of a respondent and desertion for two years. These charges would have to be proved, in undefended as well as defended, as heretofore.

But sub-clause (*a*), that since the celebration of the marriage the respondent has committed adultery *and the petitioner finds it intolerable to live with the respondent,* is not so easy to interpret. It is the latter part which is likely to cause the judge perplexity. Does it mean that the mere fact of adultery makes it intolerable for the petitioner to continue to live with the respondent? Or must there be aggravated circumstances? An amendment to clarify this ambiguity was rejected by the Standing Committee.

The wider issues in (*d*), divorce by mutual consent after two years' separation, and (*e*), right of either party to divorce after five years' separation, have been considered previously.

The root of the trouble for the judges will be the moral one. They are statute-bound to exercise equity unless Parliament decrees otherwise. Equity has been variously defined. Byrne's *Legal Dictionary* puts it thus: 'When a legal rule or remedy is capable of two interpretations or applications, one literal or restrictive, and the other calculated to make the rule or remedy operate fairly . . . the latter is called the equitable construction or remedy.'

When the discretion statement was first evolved in divorce practice, whereby a petitioner was bound to confess his own adultery, this was an equitable rule for the benefit of a respondent whose own wrongdoing might have been influenced by the petitioner's own adultery. It was also considered necessary for the proper administration of justice. But the Act purports to sweep it away, just as it is prepared to consider a petitioner's connivance at the respondent's adultery as proof of irretrievable breakdown of marriage, another example of letting a spouse take advantage of his or her own wrongdoing. Yet the obligation for the discretion confession was not recognised by statute till later.

It may be asked what has morality to do with the administration of justice in the Divorce Court? One of the best answers to this question is contained in a passage by Lord Denning, now Master of the Rolls, in his book *The Changing Law*[1]:

Many people now think that religion and law have nothing in common. The law, they say, governs our dealings with our fellows; whereas religion concerns our dealings with God. Likewise they hold that law has nothing to do with morality. It lays down rigid rules which must be obeyed without questioning whether they are right or wrong. Its function is to keep order, not to do justice.

The severance has gone much too far. Although religion, law and morals can be separated, they are still nevertheless still very much dependent on each other. Without religion there can be no morality; and without morality there can be no law.

In a later passage Lord Denning wrote:

The family is the primary social unit. The wellbeing of the whole community requires that children should, so far as possible,

[1] Stevens & Sons, 1953.

be brought up by their own parents as members of one family, with all the give and take that family life demands, and also with the security that it affords. The institution of marriage is the legal foundation of this family life. The principle of indissolubility was the binding force which cemented it. The State has abandoned the principle. Divorce has been allowed for grave causes, prescribed by law, but the consequences that were foreseen by the Church, and of which its leaders gave warning have followed.

Undeserving cases have slipped through. Collusion has not been detected. The result is that people have come to regard divorce as a matter which can be arranged between the parties. In so doing, they only too often disregard the interests of the children and pursue their own selfish ends. Every thinking person is profoundly disturbed by this state of affairs . . . The only real remedy is the growth of a strong public opinion condemning divorce. It should not be regarded, as it now is, as the private concern of the parties with which no one else has anything to do. It is the concern of everyone who has the welfare of the country at heart.

On this note one might ask: if divorce is merely the concern of the parties why in the past and in the future, because this procedure is unchanged, is it deemed necessary to petition the Crown? Why should it not be an ordinary action at common law with plaintiff and defendant, so that undefended cases should be the subject of a summons under Order XIV of the Supreme Court Rules, a rubber stamp judgment, and no questions asked?

One of the features of the Parliamentary debates which has puzzled ordinary members of the public has been the almost total silence of political leaders of all parties. Even the promoters of the Bill have acknowledged that it was a measure of outstanding social importance but only three political leaders gave their opinions, Mr Quintin Hogg and Mr Enoch Powell against, and Lord Gardiner for. When the Bill secured its first Second Reading in the House of Commons Mr Quintin Hogg made an earnest speech in opposition from the Front Bench. He said:

When we look at the provisions of clause 2 (1)(e) about the
five-year period before repudiation, one has to reflect that the
interests which we have to consider today are not merely the
children of the marriage which we are bringing to an end, but
the wisdom or unwisdom of the partners to the second marriages
bringing new children into the world . . . Marriage is a contract
leading to a status . . . The interests of persons not parties to
the arrangement are intimately concerned from the beginning.
They are the children of the marriage and the potential children,
illegitimate or legitimate, who may be born in a subsequent
union . . . How many of these irresponsible second unions—and
they are in many cases irresponsible—are actually encouraged or
achieved by reason of the availability of divorce? . . . Divorce is
a licence to remarry and form a new union. There may be an
order referring to the maintenance and custody of the children
of the first marriage, or for the maintenance of the first wife.
Until one asks to what extent are we increasing the sum of
human happiness by altering the terms of those orders, one
cannot arrive at a proper assessment of the value of the Bill.

In an article in the *Sunday Telegraph* of 22 December 1968,
Mr Peregrine Worsthorne asked whether keeping party politics
out of moral questions had any longer much sense. He wrote:

Last week's debate on the Divorce Reform Bill suggests that
there is something very peculiar about the manner in which
moral matters are now determined in this country. Here was a
moral issue of the most fundamental kind. Nothing affects the
moral quality of a society so deeply as the rules governing
marriage. No society has ever allowed the individual conscience to
decide these matters for itself. They have to be settled according
to the prevailing ideas of right and wrong; that is, according to
the moral law.

Yet a Second Reading was given to this very far-reaching new
Bill, the main effect of which is a notable move towards the
legalisation of bigamy, without one of our major political figures
expressing a view. Neither of the main parties came out officially

167

either for or against it. The pretence is that there still *is* a moral consensus, which the Government is merely heeding by giving Parliamentary time for the Bill—a consensus no longer determined by ecclesiastical authority, but by informed opinion, by the experts, by the intellectuals, by social workers. Instead of 'Ask the Archbishop', it is now 'Ask the Professors of Sociology'. Can this possibly be said to be a moral consensus of the same category as that represented by the Christian Churches? Of course it cannot. The Christian consensus was broad and deep, a genuine popular consensus. The intellectual consensus is narrow and shallow, the views of an unrepresentative minority.

Even now the Bill has become law no one can be sure that the better provisions for the financial protection of cast-off wives and children promised by the Lord Chancellor will be effective, when the Matrimonial Proceedings and Property Bill becomes law.

One result of the Divorce Reform Act seems certain. The tide of divorce will rise rapidly and may overflow.

Index

169